THOMAS KENEALLY

Level 6

Retold by Nancy Taylor
Series Editors: Andy Hopkins and Jocelyn Potter

BAL
fic

For a complete list of the titles available in the Penguin Readers series please write to your local
Pearson Education office or to: Penguin Readers Marketing Department, Pearson Education,
Edinburgh Gate, Harlow, Essex, CM20 2JE.

Contents

Introduction

He who saves the life of one man, saves the entire world.

As a happy child growing up in a middle-class German family between the wars, Oskar Schindler would never have imagined that this verse from the Talmud would guide him through the darkest days of the Second World War.

He was not an intellectual man and did not have the patience to sit quietly and analyze situations, but he learnt quickly, felt passionately and knew who to trust. When he observed how the SS treated first the Czechs in Sudetenland and then the Jews in Poland, Schindler began his own war against the Nazi system. Putting his life at risk every day, he used his impressive charm and energy to save the lives of as many Jews as possible.

Schindler's List is more than a well-written, exciting story. It is an accurate, frightening history of what happened to real people in German-occupied territories between 1939 and 1945.

Thomas Keneally was born in Australia in 1935. As a young man he spent seven years studying to become a priest, but in the end he decided to become a school teacher instead.

He began writing in 1964 and has published twenty-two novels since then. Many of his books have won literary prizes and several have been made into films, but *Schindler's Ark*, published in 1982, made him internationally famous. The novel won numerous prizes and was later renamed *Schindler's List* and filmed by Steven Spielberg. The movie won seven Oscars in 1993, including Best Picture and Best Director, and brought both Schindler's story and the story of millions of Jews in the Second World War to a mass audience.

In 1983 Keneally received the Order of Australia for his service to literature. He now lives in New South Wales with his wife, Margaret.

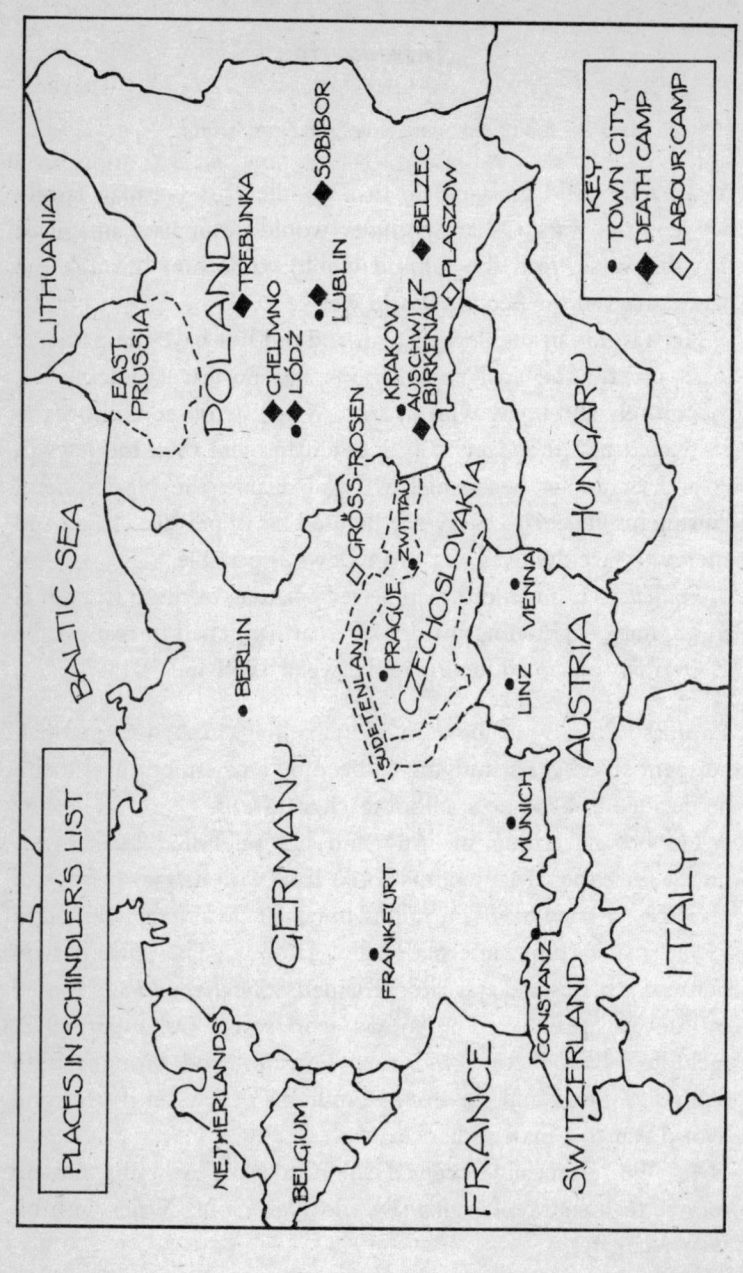

PLACES IN SCHINDLER'S LIST

Chapter 1 A Happy Child with a Bright Future

Oskar Schindler is the hero of this story, but nothing in his early life suggested that he would become a great, even a noble man.

Oskar was born on 28 April 1908 in the industrial town of Zwittau (now Suitava), where his family had lived since the beginning of the sixteenth century. In Oskar's childhood, this region was known as Sudetenland and was part of the Austrian Empire, ruled by Franz Josef. After the First World War it became part of Czechoslovakia, and later the Czech Republic.

Oskar's parents were great supporters of Franz Josef and proud to be Sudeten 'Germans'. They spoke German at home and at their jobs, and their children went to German-speaking schools. Few people in this quiet corner of Czechoslovakia objected to the way of life that the Schindlers and other Sudeten Germans had chosen for themselves.

Zwittau was a small industrial city, surrounded by hills and forests. Oskar's father, Hans Schindler, owned a factory which made farm machinery and employed about forty-five people. Oskar studied engineering in secondary school with the idea that one day he would run the factory for his father.

Herr* Schindler was a big, sociable man. He enjoyed fine wine and good tobacco and liked to spend his evenings in coffee houses, where the conversation was clever and amusing. He was the kind of man who could drive a wife to religion, and Frau Louisa Schindler practised her Roman Catholic faith with energy and sincerity. It worried her that her son stayed away from church as much as his father did.

*Herr, Frau: German for Mr and Mrs. Unlike the English titles, they can be used with other titles, such as Herr Direktor or Herr Kommandant.

In later years Oskar and his sister, Elfriede, remembered a childhood filled with sunshine. They lived in a modern house with a big garden and enjoyed being the children of a successful businessman. Oskar had an early passion for cars and began building his own motorbike as a teenager.

Some of the students at Oskar's German secondary school were from middle-class Jewish families and had fathers who were also successful businessmen. In fact, a liberal Jewish rabbi and his family lived next door to the Schindlers. Rabbi Kantor was a modern, intellectual man, proud to be both a German and a Jew, and always ready to enjoy a friendly debate about religion or politics with Herr Schindler. His sons went to school with Oskar and Elfriede, and the four children ran and played between the two gardens.

The Kantor boys were bright students, perhaps intelligent enough to become lecturers at the German University of Prague one day. But this dream changed in the mid-thirties. Rabbi Kantor had to admit that the Nazi Party* would never permit a Jew to teach at a university or to succeed as a scientist or businessman. There was certainly no type of rabbi that was acceptable to this new government either. In 1936 the Kantor family moved to Belgium, and the Schindlers never heard of them again.

History and politics meant little to Oskar as a teenager. His enthusiasm was centred around fast motorbikes, and his father encouraged this interest. In Oskar's last year at school, Hans Schindler bought his son an Italian motorbike. Then in the middle of 1928, at the beginning of Oskar's sweetest and most innocent summer, he appeared in the town square on a Moto-Guzzi, an amazing motorbike usually owned only by professional racers.

*Nazi Party: National Socialist German Workers' Party. A German political party from 1919, it dominated Germany from 1933 to 1945 under its leader, Adolf Hitler. One of the Nazis' goals was to rid German territories of all Jews.

For three months Oskar forgot about his studies and his future and entered professional motorbike races. He did very well and loved every exciting minute of this life. In his final race, in the hills on the German border, Oskar was competing against the best riders in Europe. He kept close to the leaders throughout the race and just failed to win. Even though people said he could become a champion racer, Oskar decided to end his motorbike career after that thrilling afternoon. The reason may have been economic because, by hurrying into marriage with a farmer's daughter that summer, Oskar lost the approval of his father, who was also his employer. The elder Schindler could see that Oskar was similar to him, and he worried that his son was marrying a girl like his own mother: a girl who was quiet, graceful and religious, but not very suitable for the sociable, charming and handsome Oskar.

The bride's father, a wealthy widower, was as unhappy about the marriage as Hans Schindler was. He was a gentleman-farmer who had expected Emilie, his daughter, to do better than to marry a boy on a motorbike with no money of his own. The bride, according to the custom of the time, agreed to bring a large sum of money into the marriage. Most of this money was never paid, however, because Emilie's father did not believe that Oskar would settle down and be a good husband to his only child.

Emilie, on the other hand, was delighted to leave her small village and her father's old-fashioned household, where she had to act as hostess to him and his boring friends. She was enthusiastic about moving into an apartment in Zwittau with her tall, handsome young husband. However, Emilie's dream of a happy marriage did not last long. Oskar followed his father's example and forgot about his wife in the evenings, staying in cafés like a single man, talking to girls who were neither religious nor quiet.

Hans Schindler's business went bankrupt in 1935, and soon afterwards he left his wife and found an apartment on his own.

Oskar hated his father for abandoning his mother and refused to speak to him. The son seemed blind to the fact that his treatment of Emilie was already following the same pattern.

Meanwhile, even though the world's economy was suffering, Oskar managed to get a good job. He had good business contacts, he had a background in engineering and he was good company. These qualities made him the perfect man to become the sales manager of Moravian Electrotechnic. He began travelling a lot, which reminded him of his time as a motorbike racer, and which gave him an excuse to stay away from his responsibilities in Zwittau.

By the time of his mother's funeral in the late 1930s, Oskar, like many young Czech Germans, was wearing a swastika, the badge of the Nazi Party, on the collar of his suit. He was still not interested in politics, but Oskar was a salesman. When he went into the office of a German company manager wearing the swastika, he got the orders that he wanted.

Oskar was a busy, successful salesman, but he could feel something even more exciting than money in the air. In 1938, in the month before the German army entered Sudetenland and made it part of the Third Reich,* Oskar sensed that history was being made, and he wanted to be part of the action.

But, just as quickly as he had become disappointed in marriage, Oskar became disappointed with the Nazi Party. When German soldiers captured Sudetenland, Oskar was shocked by their rough treatment of the Czech population and the seizing of property. By March of 1939 he had quietly turned away from the Party.

Oskar was not ready to reject Hitler's grand plans completely at this time. In 1939 it was still not clear what kind of men would lead Germany forward. One evening that autumn at a party near

*Third Reich: Germany during the period of Nazi rule from 1933 to 1945

the Polish border, the hostess, a client and friend, introduced Oskar to a sociable, clever German named Eberhard Gebauer. The two men talked about business and the political situation in Europe. After several glasses of wine Gebauer explained that he worked for German military intelligence and asked Oskar if he could help them in Poland. With his charm and contacts, Oskar would be a useful agent for collecting military and industrial information for the German government.

Oskar agreed to the proposal for two reasons. First, it meant that he would not have to serve in the army, and second, he almost certainly approved of Germany's plan to seize Poland. He believed in Hitler's goals as he understood them at that time, but he still hoped that there would be civilized ways to achieve them. He hoped that decent men like Gebauer, not men like Himmler* and the SS,† would guide Germany.

Oskar was praised in the following months for his useful and thorough reports. He was good at persuading people to talk to him over a fine dinner with an expensive bottle of wine or two. As he did this work and continued as a salesman, Oskar also discovered that Krakow, the ancient centre of cultural life in Poland, offered many possibilities to an ambitious young businessman.

Chapter 2 War Brings Troubles and Opportunities

Germany invaded Poland from the west on 1 September 1939. The USSR invaded Poland from the east on 17 September. The Second World War had begun.

*Heinrich Himmler (1900–1945): German Nazi leader who directed the SS and Gestapo forces and ran the concentration camps in the Second World War
† SS: the special military and security unit of the Nazi Party

By the seventh week of German rule, the inhabitants of Krakow were struggling to make sense of the orders that arrived daily from the authorities in Berlin. Poles had to exist on the rations allowed to them; they had to do whatever jobs they were given.

But the Jews of Poland, who represented one in every eleven of the population, began to realize that their situation was particularly dangerous. Already they had to declare their Jewish origins and carry Jewish identity cards. As sub-humans, as the Germans insultingly called them, they received only half of the official rations given to non-Jewish Poles. The German administration insisted that all Jews must register with the appropriate government office by 24 November of that year. In this environment, it was obviously wise for a Jew to be careful of what he said and did.

One Polish Jew who understood what was happening better than most people in Krakow was Itzhak Stern, chief accountant at J C Buchheister and Company and an expert on Jewish law and religious texts. One day in October his new German bosses called him into the director's office as usual. They understood very little about the factory they were now running and relied on Stern to guide them.

The thin, intellectual Jew entered the big office and was introduced to Oskar Schindler and Ingrid, a beautiful young Sudeten German who had recently become the manager of a Jewish tool factory. They were an elegant, stylish couple, full of confidence and clearly in love with one another. They would go far under this new system.

'Herr Schindler,' the German director said, 'this is Itzhak Stern. He understands this factory and can also help you with information about other local industries.'

According to the rules of the day, Stern said, 'I have to tell you, sir, that I am a Jew.'

'Well,' Schindler confessed with a smile, 'I'm a German. So let's talk business.'

It's easy for you to be friendly, thought the accountant, *but I must still live by your rules*. Nevertheless, Stern understood history and trusted that, even though conditions would probably get worse, the Jews would survive in Poland. As a race, they had learnt how to deal with foreign rulers over many centuries. And anyway, young businessmen like Oskar Schindler still needed people with experience, whether they were Jews or not.

When Stern was alone with Oskar and Ingrid, Oskar began the conversation. 'I would be grateful if you could tell me about some of the local businesses.'

'With respect, Herr Schindler,' said Stern, 'perhaps you should speak to the German officials who are now in charge of business in Krakow.'

Schindler laughed and said, 'They're thieves and rule-makers. I don't like having to follow a lot of rules.'

So Stern and the young industrialist began to talk. Stern had friends or relatives in every factory in Krakow and understood how the economy worked. Schindler was impressed and finally asked the question he had come to ask: 'What do you know about a company called Rekord?'

'It went bankrupt before the Germans arrived. It made enamelware, but was badly managed,' Stern reported.

'I have the financial statements for the company's last five years in business. Can you give me your opinion of them?' asked Schindler as one businessman to another.

Stern looked carefully at this friendly German. Like many Jews, he had the gift of knowing in his bones who was a good non-Jew. He began to sense that it might be important to be connected with Oskar Schindler; he might be able to offer a kind of safety.

'It's a good business,' Stern continued. 'And, with the kind of machinery it has, there's the possibility of military contracts.'

'Exactly,' Schindler replied. 'The German government is looking for Polish factories that can produce army equipment:

pots, dishes and spoons for the soldiers. With my background, I understand the kind of company we're talking about.'

Stern sensed that he could be honest with the young German. 'I can help you with the legal work. You should rent the property with the option to buy.' Then, more quietly, he added, 'There will be rules about who you can employ.'

Schindler laughed. 'How do you know so much about the authorities' intentions?'

'We are still permitted to read German newspapers,' said Stern. Actually, he had read documents from the German government that he had seen on the desks of his new bosses. He knew that one of the aims of the Third Reich was to get rid of all Jewish owners, then all Jewish bosses and, finally, all Jewish workers.

As the two men left the office, Schindler became philosophical and began talking about the fact that Christianity had its roots in Judaism. Maybe he was reminded of his boyhood friends, the Kantor brothers. Stern had written articles about religion in serious journals and quickly realized that Oskar's knowledge of religion and philosophy was not very deep, but that his feelings were sincere. A friendship began to form between the two men.

Towards the end of their conversation Oskar said, 'In times like these, it must be difficult for a priest to tell people that their Father in Heaven cares about the death of every little bird. I'd hate to be a priest today when a human life doesn't have the value of a packet of cigarettes.'

'You are right, Herr Schindler,' said Stern. 'The story you are referring to from the Bible can be summarized by a line from the Talmud* which says that he who saves the life of one man, saves the entire world.'

'Of course, of course,' answered the German.

*Talmud: the most important book of holy writings for Jews

Rightly or wrongly, Itzhak Stern always believed that these words from the Talmud guided Oskar Schindler throughout the next five years.

◆

Schindler met Itzhak Stern by accident because he kept his eyes and ears open for people who might be useful to him. He met another Krakow Jew, Leopold Pfefferberg, by chance too.

Like other important Germans in the Polish city in 1939, Oskar had been given a fine apartment by the German housing authorities. It had previously been owned by a Jewish family by the name of Nussbaum who the authorities had ordered to move out without paying them for the apartment or its furniture.

Years later, several of Oskar's friends from the war claimed that he searched Krakow for the Nussbaum family in 1939 and gave them enough money to escape to Yugoslavia. This kind of generous behaviour was typical of Schindler. In fact, some people said that being generous became a disease in him – a disease because he was always in danger of dying from it.

Back in 1939 Oskar liked his big new apartment very much, but he wanted to decorate it in a more modern style. He heard that Mrs Mina Pfefferberg was the best interior decorator in Krakow, so he went to see her.

Mrs Pfefferberg and her husband were still living in their own apartment, but they feared a visit from the Gestapo,* announcing that the Pfefferberg home now belonged to a German army officer or businessman. (In fact, their apartment was taken from them by the Gestapo before the end of 1939.) When Mrs Pfefferberg heard a knock one morning in October, looked through a crack and saw a tall, well-dressed German with a

*Gestapo: the Nazi secret police; the SS and the Gestapo controlled the concentration camps.

swastika pinned to his suit, she thought that day had arrived. She looked at her 27-year-old son, Leopold, with alarm in her eyes.

'Mother, don't worry. The man is not wearing a Gestapo uniform. He's probably looking for me,' said Leopold calmly. He had been an officer in the Polish army until their defeat in September and, after he had been captured, managed to avoid being sent to Germany. Perhaps the Germans had found him now. Recently he had been surviving by buying and selling on the black market because he had not been allowed to return to his real job as a physical education teacher. In fact Jewish schools were closed soon after this time.

'Answer the door, Mother,' whispered Leopold. 'I'll hide in the kitchen and hear what he wants. If he makes trouble for you, I've got my gun.'

Mrs Pfefferberg nervously opened the door.

'You're Mrs Pfefferberg?' the German asked. 'You were recommended to me by Herr Nussbaum. I have just taken over an apartment near here and would like to have it redecorated.'

Mrs Pfefferberg could not manage a reply, even though the German was speaking politely. Leopold stepped into the room and spoke for her. 'Please, come in, sir.'

'Thank you. I am Oskar Schindler. My wife will be coming here from Czechoslovakia,' he explained, 'and I'd like to have my new apartment ready for her.'

With her strong, healthy son beside her, Mrs Pfefferberg relaxed and began to talk to Schindler as a client, discussing fabrics and colours and costs. After it was settled that Mrs Pfefferberg would do the work, Oskar turned to Leopold and said, 'Could you visit me at my apartment one day and discuss other business matters? Maybe you can tell me how to get local products when the shops are empty. For example, where would a man find such an elegant blue shirt as yours?'

Leopold knew that this man wanted more than a good blue shirt; his business sense told him that he could make some profitable deals with this customer. He answered, 'Herr Schindler, these shirts are hard to find and they're extremely expensive. But give me your size and I'll see what I can do.'

Oskar expected to be charged a very high price for the shirts, but he was sure that this Jew would be useful to him. In fact, Leopold became one of Oskar's most reliable sources of black market luxuries, and, as the years passed, those luxuries kept Oskar in business time after time.

◆

By December of 1939 it had become clear that the Germans would not be leaving Krakow very soon, but Oskar, and even many Polish Jews, continued to hope that the situation would be better in the spring. After all, the Jews told themselves, Germany is a civilized nation.

Through his contacts in the German police and military, Oskar heard troubling rumours. He learnt that the SS would carry out their first *Aktion** in a Jewish suburb of Krakow on 4 December. He went to the Buchheister offices and dropped hints for Stern, but this was the first *Aktion* and few believed it would happen.

The SS plan was to carry the war against the Jews from door to door. They broke into apartments and emptied desks and wardrobes; they took rings off fingers and watches out of pockets. A girl who would not give up her fur coat had her arm broken. A boy who wanted to keep his skis was shot.

There were worse events occurring in other parts of the city, being carried out by a group of German soldiers with special duties, known as the Einsatz Group. From the beginning of the

*Aktion: a military operation against private citizens by the SS

war, they had understood that Hitler's plan meant the extinction of the Jewish race, and they were willing to take extreme steps to achieve this goal.

While the SS were busy with their first *Aktion* in Krakow, Einsatz soldiers entered a fourteenth-century synagogue in another Jewish neighbourhood, where traditional Jews were at prayer. Their companions went from apartment to apartment and drove the less religious Jews into the synagogue too.

The Einsatz leader ordered each Jew to spit on the holy Jewish texts at the front of the hall or be shot. One man, described by people in the neighbourhood as a gangster with no interest in religion, refused to spit on the book.

'I've done a lot of bad things in my life,' the crook said, 'but I won't do that.' The Einsatz men shot him first. Then they shot the rest of the Jews and set fire to the place, destroying the oldest of all Polish synagogues.

But higher up the ladder of Nazi authority, men were discussing the weakness of a plan that required German soldiers to kill Jews one at a time, or even in small groups. They were looking for a faster, more efficient method of solving the Jewish 'problem' in Europe. Scientists eventually found a technological solution: a chemical named Zyklon B that could be used to kill hundreds of Jews at a time in secret sites throughout the German empire.

Chapter 3 Adjusting to a World at War

Oskar Schindler continued to consult with Itzhak Stern throughout 1939. Soon his plans were in place to open Deutsche Email Fabrik, or DEF, in the buildings of the former Rekord Company in the suburb of Zablocie. The factory would produce enamelware for the kitchens of Poland and for the German army. Oskar had the site, the experience and the right contacts in the

German administration, but he needed cash. Stern introduced him to Abraham Bankier, a Jew and former office manager at Rekord.

On 23 November 1939, all Jewish money and accounts in Polish banks had been frozen by the Germans. Jews could not touch any of their cash, but some of the rich Jewish businessmen had already put their money elsewhere, often in diamonds, gold or pieces of art. Bankier met with a group of these men, and they agreed to invest money in Oskar's factory in exchange for a certain quantity of enamelware over the next year. They knew that manufactured goods would be more useful to them than cash.

The men left their meeting with Bankier without a written contract. Such contracts were not considered legal documents in those days, but in the end the Jews found that they had made a good deal. Schindler was honest and generous; the Jews who put money into DEF received everything they were promised.

When DEF opened, Oskar employed forty-five workers and made only enamelware. At the beginning of 1940, to no one's surprise, the factory began to receive contracts from the army. Oskar had worked hard to make friends with men who had influence in government offices and in the army, entertaining them at the best restaurants and clubs and remembering birthdays and other special celebrations with wine, carpets, jewellery, furniture and baskets of luxury food.

After asking for and receiving permission to expand his business, Oskar bought new machines and opened more of the old buildings, with one section producing pots and pans and another producing military equipment for the German army. By the summer of 1940, DEF had 250 employees of which 150 were Jews. Many of them had been introduced to Oskar by Stern, and DEF began to win a reputation as a safe place for Jews to work.

The beautiful Victoria Klonowska was a Polish secretary in DEF's front office, and Oskar began a romantic relationship with her. Ingrid, his German girlfriend, lived with him in his new apartment. Emilie, his wife, continued to live in Zwittau. These three women obviously knew about each other, and about the other occasional girlfriends that Oskar was seen with around the city. Oskar never tried to make a secret of his love life, and because he did not lie to any of the three women, traditional lovers' arguments never developed.

Victoria Klonowska was blonde and very attractive and wore clothes that were different from those of the depressed, grey women on the streets of Krakow. For Christmas Oskar bought her a ridiculous little white dog which perfectly suited her fresh, fashion-magazine style. But Oskar appreciated her for more than just her beauty: she was also efficient, clever and persuasive. She knew how to talk to important people and how to keep them on Oskar's side. She also knew Krakow well and could recommend people and places that met her boss's needs.

Oskar took Nazi leaders and other German officials to the old, traditional Hotel Krakovia, where they could eat heavy meals and drink expensive German wines while listening to old-fashioned music from Vienna. But he wanted a good night-club where he could take his real friends, and Victoria knew the perfect place. She recommended a jazz club which was popular with students and young lecturers from the university and which would not attract SS men or Nazi supporters.

At the end of 1939 Oskar organized a Christmas party at the jazz club for a group of friends. These men were all Germans who were away from their homes, and they all had doubts about some of the goals of the Nazi administration. Oskar had done business with each of them, and he had enjoyed long sociable evenings in their company.

Eberhard Gebauer from military intelligence, who had first sent Oskar to Poland, was among the party. Oskar's work for Gebauer had continued, even including reports on the behaviour of the SS in Krakow. Gebauer invited the other guests to raise their glasses.

'I ask you to raise your glasses to our good friend, Oskar Schindler, and to the success of his enamelware factory. If DEF makes a lot of money, Herr Schindler will throw a lot more parties – and his are the best parties in the world!'

The men around the table shouted, 'To Oskar!'

But after a fine meal and a few more speeches, the talk turned to the subject that none of them could forget: the Jews.

'We spent the day at the railway station, trying to decide what to do with boxcar after boxcar full of Jews and Poles,' complained Herman Toffel, a young German policeman. 'We're at war, but the whole railway system is being used to send all the Jews from the German territories to us. How is the German army travelling? By bicycle?'

Soon everyone in Poland would get used to the sight of trains packed with human beings who had been pushed into the boxcars by lying SS men with the promise that their luggage would be waiting for them at the other end. But at Oskar's 1939 Christmas party people were still surprised by this idea.

'They call it "concentration",' said Toffel. 'That's the word in the official documents. I call it a waste of our time. What are we supposed to do with more Jews?'

'The men at the top say that they are going to get rid of all of the Jews in Krakow as soon as possible,' said a military man. 'They may allow five or six thousand Jewish workers with special skills to stay, but I don't know what they're going to do with the rest of them, not to mention all the new arrivals.'

'Maybe the Judenrat★ will find work for them,' suggested Gebauer. 'Their leader has given my office a plan for using Jewish labour. They are willing to carry coal, sweep streets, dig ditches – anything to make themselves useful.'

★Judenrat: a Jewish council set up in each Jewish community by order of the German administration

15

'They'll cooperate to avoid something worse,' added another of the guests. 'That's how they've always survived.'

'But this time things are going to be different. They don't have any idea how to save themselves from the plans of the SS,' said Gebauer rather sadly.

Oskar could see from the faces of the men at this table that they did not hate Jews, and he felt a sense of relief in their company. These men were his friends, and in the future they would also help him to carry out his own plans.

Oskar did not spend all of his time in restaurants and clubs. He worked very hard during DEF's first year in business – harder than he had ever worked in his life – but it was worth it because DEF was making a fortune for him. Part of Oskar's satisfaction came from the fact that he was employing a lot more people and was making a lot more money than his father had ever done.

The only thing that slowed down the work in the factory was the weather. On bad days the SS men stopped Jews on their way to work and made them clear the streets and pavements of snow. Sometimes as many as 125 workers failed to arrive at the factory on a winter morning. Oskar went to SS headquarters to complain to his friend Herman Toffel.

'I have military contracts,' explained Oskar, 'and DEF is part of an essential industry. My products will help Germany win the war, but my workers must arrive at my factory on time every day.'

'Oskar, these SS men don't care about contracts or essential industries. They want to see Jews working like slaves for them. They're causing problems for every factory in Krakow.'

Oskar left thinking about what Toffel had said. A factory owner must have control over his workers; they must not be prevented from coming to work. It was an industrial principle, but also a moral one. Oskar would apply it to the limit at DEF.

◆

As his employees worked on DEF's military contracts at the beginning of 1941, Oskar began to hear rumours that a ghetto was planned for the Jews in Krakow. He hurried to Itzhak Stern's office to warn him.

'Oh yes, Herr Schindler,' said Stern calmly, 'we have heard about this plan. Some people are even looking forward to the ghetto because we'll be together inside, and the enemy will be outside. We can run our own affairs without people throwing stones at us or spitting on us. The walls of the ghetto will be the final step that the Germans will take against us.'

On the same day, Schindler heard two Germans talking in a bar. 'All Jews have to be inside the ghetto by 20 March. Things will be better without Jews living near us.'

'Better for the Poles too,' added his friend. 'They hate the Jews as much as we do. They blame them for everything that has gone wrong in Poland in this century. When I came here in 1939, the Poles wanted to help us punish the Jews. Maybe even the Jews will be happier if they're separated from the Poles and from us.'

Many Jews agreed with this opinion even though they knew that life in the ghetto would be very hard. The ghetto itself would be small, and they would have to live in crowded rooms, sharing their space with families who had different customs and habits. They would have to have an official labour card to be able to leave the ghetto for work, which they would no longer be paid for. They would have to survive on their rations.

But there would be definite rules, and the Jews believed they would be able to adjust to them in a place where their lives could again be organized and calm. For some older Jews the ghetto also represented a kind of homecoming, and like Jews over the centuries in other ghettos, they would drink coffee together, even if they could not have cream in it, and they would enjoy being Jewish among Jews.

By March, as he drove one of his four luxury cars from his apartment to his factory each morning, Oskar saw Jewish families carrying or pushing their odd bits and pieces into the ghetto. He assumed that this was how Jewish families had arrived in Krakow over five hundred years before.

For two weeks, the Jews walked between the apartments and the ghetto with their beds, their chairs, their pots and pans. They had hidden their jewellery and their fur coats under piles of pillows and blankets. As they walked through the streets, crowds of Poles threw mud and shouted, 'The Jews are going! Goodbye, Jews!'

An official from the Judenrat Housing Office met each family at the ghetto gate and directed them to their room. On 20 March the move was complete, and for the moment, the Jews were at rest.

Twenty-three-year-old Edith Liebgold now lived in one room with her mother and her young baby. When Krakow had fallen to the Germans eighteen months before, her husband had become severely depressed. One day he had walked into the forest and never come back.

On her second day inside the ghetto, Edith saw an SS truck stop in the square and take people away to clean the streets. It was not the work that Edith was afraid of, but she had heard rumours that the trucks usually returned with fewer people than when they left.

Next morning Edith went to the Jewish Employment Office with a group of her friends. She hoped to be able to get a job at night when her mother could look after the baby. The office was crowded – everyone wanted a job in essential industry and a labour card. Edith and her friends were talking and laughing together when a serious-looking man in a suit and tie came over to them. He had been attracted by their noise and energy.

'Excuse me,' said Abraham Bankier. 'Instead of waiting, there is an enamelware factory in Zablocie which needs ten healthy women to work nights. It's outside the ghetto so you'll get labour cards. You'll be able to get things you need on the outside.'

He waited and let the girls think for a minute or two.

'Is the work hard?' asked one girl.

'Not heavy work,' he assured them. 'And they'll teach you on the job. The owner is a good man.'

'A German?'

'Of course,' said Bankier, 'but one of the good ones.'

'Does he beat his workers?' asked Edith.

'No, never,' answered Bankier. 'And he gives them good thick soup and bread every day.'

That night Edith and her friends arrived at DEF and were taken upstairs to the director's office by Bankier. When he opened the door, the girls saw Herr Schindler sitting behind a huge desk, smoking a cigarette. The girls were impressed by the tall, handsome figure who stood to greet them. His clean, shiny hair was between blonde and light brown. In his expensive suit and silk tie, he looked like a man on his way to the theatre or a smart dinner party. He looked, in fact, like Hitler's perfect German.

'I want to welcome you,' he told them in Polish. 'If you work here, then you will live through the war – you'll be safe. Now I must say good night to you. Mr Bankier will explain your jobs.'

How could anyone make this promise to them? Was he a god? Maybe so, because they all believed him. Edith and the other girls began their nights at DEF in a happy dream, remembering Herr Schindler's magic words. If he was wrong, then there was nothing good in the world: no God, no bread, no kindness. But he was their best hope, and they continued to believe him.

◆

Just before Easter Oskar left Krakow and drove west through the forests to Zwittau to visit Emilie and the rest of his family. For a few days he wanted to spend money on them and enjoy their admiration of his expensive car and his success in Poland.

Emilie was pleased to have Oskar at home for the holiday and looked forward to attending church with her husband and walking through Zwittau together like an old-fashioned couple. But their evenings alone in their own house were formal and polite rather than happy and romantic. There was always the question of whether or not Emilie should move to Krakow. Wasn't it her duty as a good Catholic wife to be living with her husband? But Emilie would not consider moving to Poland unless Oskar gave up his girlfriends and protected her reputation as his wife.

Unfortunately they could not discuss their situation openly, and so they continued to follow their old ways. After dinner each evening Oskar excused himself and went to a café in the main square to see old friends, most of whom were now soldiers. After a few drinks on one occasion a friend asked, 'Oskar, why isn't a strong young fellow like you in the army?'

'Part of an essential industry,' responded Oskar. 'Someone has to supply the German army with the things it needs.'

They laughed and told stories from before the war. Then one of the friends got serious. 'Oskar, your father is here. He's sick and lonely. Why don't you have a word with him?'

'No, I'm going home,' answered Oskar quickly, but the friend pushed him into his chair as another led Hans Schindler over.

'How are you, Oskar?' asked the elder Schindler in a weak voice.

Oskar was surprised to see how small and ill this proud old man looked. Oskar knew from his own marriage that relationships could follow laws of their own; he understood now why his father had left his mother. He put his arms around the old man and kissed him on the cheek. His soldier friends, who had once been motorbikers like Oskar, cheered.

Back in Krakow, Oskar began to receive letters from his father, always on the same topic: Hitler would not win the war because, in the end, the Americans and Russians would crush his evil empire. Oskar smiled at his father's lack of loyalty to the German leader, then sent him another cheque to make up for the lost years.

◆

Of course life in the ghetto could never match the optimistic dream that many Jews had in March of 1941. Life changed when the administration of the ghetto passed from the control of the local German authorities, who relied on help from the Judenrat and the ghetto's own police force, to Gestapo Section 4B, which was in charge of religion. This change occurred in the other big Jewish ghettos in the cities of Warsaw and Lódz too. In Krakow SS boss Julian Scherner now made all the rules for his ghetto, and life became even harder for the Jews under his administration.

Some young Jewish men who had never had any power or position in the Jewish community took jobs in the new administration and learnt to make money by accepting bribes and making lists of uncooperative Jews for the SS. They were happy to obey Herr Scherner if it meant more power and more bread for them and their families. But would their luck last? Germany invaded Russia in 1941, and the nature of SS planning changed. The entire Nazi army was now preparing for a long war and carrying out Hitler's plan to make Germany a racially pure nation.

Oskar visited the ghetto in April to order two rings from a jeweller and to have a look around. He was shocked by the crowded conditions and the offensive smells, even though the women worked all day trying to keep the ghetto clean and free of lice in order to prevent the spread of infectious diseases. The situation made Oskar think about the land behind his factory. He knew how to get as much wood as he wanted, and he began to wonder if he could get permission to build on this land.

For Oskar Schindler 1941 was a fast, busy, but still almost easy year. He worked long hours, went to parties at the Hotel

Krakovia, to drinking evenings at the jazz club and to romantic dinners with Victoria Klonowska. When the leaves began to fall, he wondered where the year had gone.

Then, near the end of the year, he was arrested. Perhaps a Polish shipping clerk or a German engineer had reported him to the Gestapo for breaking one of the many new rules. But more likely, it was because of Oskar's black market trading. You could never predict how people would react to success.

'You must bring your business books with you,' ordered one of the young Gestapo men who had come to arrest him.

'Exactly what books do you want?' asked Oskar, quickly realizing that these boys had not arrested many people before.

'Cash books,' said the other boy. Then the two of them went back to the outer office when the beautiful Miss Klonowska offered them coffee. Oskar got his accounts and made a list of names.

'Miss Klonowska,' said Oskar when he came out of his office, 'please cancel these meetings for tomorrow.' He handed her a piece of paper, which was actually a list of people with influence. With friends like these Oskar felt confident that he would not disappear forever behind the gates of the SS jail.

At SS headquarters Oskar was left at the desk of an older German. 'Herr Schindler,' said the official, 'please sit down. We are investigating all companies that are manufacturing products for the war effort.' Oskar did not believe the man, but he nodded to show that he understood. 'It is the duty of every factory owner to concentrate on helping our army.'

'Of course,' Oskar agreed.

'You live very well,' said the official. 'And we need to know that all of your money comes from legal contracts. We will have to keep you here while we examine your books.'

Oskar smiled and said, 'My dear sir, whoever gave you my name is a fool and is wasting your time. But, I assure you, when

Herr Scherner and I are laughing about this over a glass of wine, I will tell him that you treated me very politely.'

Oskar was then taken to a comfortable bedroom with its own bathroom and toilet. Soon there was a knock at the door, and Oskar received a small suitcase that Victoria had brought for him. It contained a bottle of whisky, some books, clean clothes and a few small luxuries. Later, a guard brought him an excellent supper with a good bottle of wine.

Next morning the official from the night before visited him. 'Herr Schindler, we have looked at your books, and we have received a number of telephone calls. It is clear that anyone who has such a close relationship with Herr Scherner and other important men is doing his best for the war effort.'

Downstairs Victoria Klonowska was waiting for him, happy that her telephone calls had worked, and that Oskar was leaving the death house without a scratch. But, as he kissed Victoria, Oskar suspected that this would not be the last time the Gestapo would call him in to ask questions about his business.

Chapter 4 Mercy Is Forgotten

Late one afternoon in 1942, when the rest of the family were at work, Mrs Clara Dresner heard a knock at the door of her family's crowded room in the ghetto. She hesitated – life was too uncertain to allow people to be friendly – but she knew there would be trouble if she ignored an official at her door. But instead of someone from the Judenrat, or even an SS officer, Mrs Dresner was surprised to see two Polish peasants and Genia, the daughter of her cousin, Eva.

Genia's parents had left her in the country with these poor farmers because they believed she would be safe there, but now even the countryside was as dangerous as the ghetto. The old Polish couple were very fond of the little girl and had treated her like a special grandchild, but neither they nor Genia were safe while the SS offered cash for every Jew who was betrayed.

Genia, always dressed in the red cap, red coat and small red boots which the peasants had lovingly given her, settled into her new life and did as she was told without question. Mrs Dresner's only concern was how strangely careful the three-year-old was about what she said, who she looked at and how she reacted to any movements around her.

The Dresner family tried to make conversation about 'Redcap's' real parents because they wanted the little girl to relax and feel at home with them. The parents had been hiding in the countryside too, but now planned to return to the relative safety of the Krakow ghetto. The child nodded as Danka, Mrs Dresner's teenage daughter, talked, but she kept quiet.

'I used to go shopping for dresses with your mother, Eva. Then we would go to a lovely tea shop and have delicious cakes. Eva always let me have hot chocolate too.'

Genia did not smile or look at anyone. 'Miss, you are mistaken,' she said. 'My mother's name is not Eva. It's Jasha.' She gave the names of the other people in her fictional family and explained where she was from. The Dresners frowned at each other but understood that this false history, which the peasants had taught her, might save her life one day.

◆

It was 28 April 1942, Oskar Schindler's thirty-fourth birthday, and he celebrated like a rich, successful businessman – loudly and expensively. A party atmosphere spread throughout the departments of DEF as Oskar provided rare white bread with the workers' soup and plenty of wine for his engineers, accountants and office workers. He passed out cigarettes and cake, and later a small group of Polish and Jewish men and women, representing the factory workers, entered the director's office to give him their best wishes.

Oskar, feeling very happy on his special day, shook hands and even kissed one of the girls.

That afternoon someone reported Herr Schindler to the authorities with a charge more serious than making money on the black market. This time Oskar was accused of a racial crime; no one could deny that he was a Jew-kisser.

He was arrested on 29 April and rushed off to Montelupich prison, an even more frightening place than Pomorska prison, where he had been taken previously. Oskar knew that he could not expect a civilized chat with an SS officer or a comfortable bedroom and good food at Montelupich. As he was led into a small dark cell with two narrow beds and two buckets on the floor – one for water and one for waste – Oskar just hoped that he would get out of this place alive and unharmed.

The door was locked behind him and after Oskar's eyes adjusted to the darkness, he realized he was not alone.

'Welcome, sir,' said an SS officer. Oskar was careful now. It was likely that this man was here to spy on him, but with nothing else to do, the two Germans eventually began to talk. Oskar acted surprised by the man's complaints against the SS – they were cruel, greedy murderers – but he was determined not to share his own opinions of them. He desperately wanted a drink; a certain amount of alcohol would make the time go faster and make his companion seem more normal.

Oskar banged on the cell bars and called for a guard. 'Is it possible to order five bottles of whisky? Here's the money.'

'Five bottles, sir?' asked the guard.

'Yes, my friend and I would like a bottle each as we're enjoying a rare opportunity for good conversation. I hope that you and your colleagues will accept the other bottles as a gift from me. And could I ask you to call my secretary and give her this list of names? I'm sure a man in your position has the power to make a routine phone call for a prisoner.'

'Are you crazy?' asked the SS officer when the guard had walked away. 'Bribing a guard is more dangerous than kissing a Jew!'

'We'll see,' said Oskar calmly, but he was frightened.

The whisky arrived and helped Oskar through his five anxious days in Montelupich. In the end his important friends got him released again, but before he left, he was called into the office of Rolf Czurda, head of the Krakow Special Duty groups.

'Oskar,' said Czurda, as an old friend, 'we give you those Jewish girls to work in your factory. You should kiss us, not them.'

'You're right, but it was my birthday.'

Czurda shook his head. 'Oskar, don't be a fool. The Jews don't have a future, I assure you. The extinction of the Jews is part of our official programme, and your important friends might not be able to save you if something like this happens again.'

◆

By the summer of 1942 any idea of the ghetto being a small but permanent community had gone. There was no longer a post office, a newspaper, a restaurant or even a school. The Nazis made it clear that the ghetto would not be there for long.

Everyone in the ghetto had to have a yellow identity card with a photo and a large blue 'J' for Jew. If you were lucky, you would get the *Blauschein*, or blue stamp, attached to your card to prove that you had an essential job outside the ghetto. Without the *Blauschein*, life became even riskier than before.

Leopold Pfefferberg continued to live by doing favours for Oskar, by buying and selling on the black market and by teaching the children of Symche Spira, chief of the Jewish ghetto police. Because he had this job, Pfefferberg expected to get the *Blauschein* with no trouble when he went to the Labour Office, but the clerks refused to give him the stamp. 'Teacher' was not an approved profession for a Jew, and no one wanted to listen to Pfefferberg's arguments about why he was an important worker.

As he came out of the office Pfefferberg was stopped by a group of German Security Police, who asked to see his identity card.

'No *Blauschein*? You join that line. Understand, Jew?' shouted one of the policemen.

Pfefferberg began to argue again, but was pushed into a line of people who, like him, did not have the precious blue stamp. When the line had grown to more than a hundred, it was marched around the corner into a yard where hundreds more people were already waiting. At fairly regular intervals, a policeman would enter the yard with a list and take a group of people to the railway station. Most people tried to stand at the edge of the yard, to stay away from the police, but Pfefferberg stayed at the front, near the gate.

Beside the guards' hut he saw a thin, sad-looking teenager in a Jewish ghetto police uniform. He was the brother of one of Pfefferberg's students. The boy looked up. 'Mr Pfefferberg, sir,' he whispered with respect, 'what are you doing here?'

'It's nonsense,' said Pfefferberg, 'but I haven't got a blue stamp.'

'Follow me, sir,' the boy said quietly. He led the former teacher to a senior officer and lied, 'This is Herr Pfefferberg from the Judenrat. He has been visiting relatives.' Without looking up, the officer waved Pfefferberg through the gate.

He could not turn and thank the teenager with sad eyes and a thin neck for saving his life without putting both the boy and himself in danger. Instead Pfefferberg rushed straight back to the Labour Office and used his charm to talk the girl behind the desk into giving him a *Blauschein*. When he came out, he was no longer a teacher with a good education. His identity card now said he was a metal polisher, an essential worker.

◆

Early one morning the following week, one of Oskar's office girls phoned the director before he had left his apartment.

'Herr Schindler, there's an emergency. I saw Mr Bankier and about a dozen more of our workers being marched out of the ghetto towards the train station when I was coming to work.'

Oskar hurried to the station and found the railway yard full of boxcars and the station crowded with people from the ghetto. He was shocked because he knew what it meant: the Jews in the yard were there for their final journey.

'Have you seen Bankier?' Oskar asked the first person he recognized, a jeweller from the ghetto.

'He's already in one of the boxcars, Herr Schindler.'

'Where are they taking you?'

'To a labour camp, they say. Near Lublin. Probably no worse than here,' said the jeweller. Oskar gave the man a pack of cigarettes and some money from his pocket before hurrying off.

Oskar remembered an invitation for bids for the construction of crematoria in a camp near Lublin in an SS publication the previous year. Even in the summer of 1942 Oskar did not want to guess at the connection between the people in this railway yard and those very large ovens. Instead he concentrated on Bankier and rushed along the boxcars calling out his name.

A young SS officer stopped him and asked for his official pass.

'I'm looking for my workers,' Schindler insisted. 'This is crazy. I have military contracts, and I need my workers in order to meet the needs of the German army.'

'You can't have them back,' said the young man. 'They're on the list.' The officer knew the rules: everyone became equal when their name was on the list.

'I don't want to argue about the list,' said Oskar. 'Where is your senior officer?'

Oskar walked up to the young man's superior, mentioned the names of a few important friends and ended by saying, 'I believe I can guarantee that you will be in southern Russia by next week.'

The senior officer told the driver to delay leaving the station, then he and the other officer hurried alongside the train with Oskar. At last they found Bankier and a dozen DEF workers in a boxcar near the end of the train. The door was unlocked and Oskar's employees quietly jumped down.

Schindler thanked the senior officer and began to follow his workers, but the SS man stopped him. 'Sir,' he said, 'it makes no difference to us. We'll put another dozen Jews on the train. Do you really think your workers are important? It's the inconvenience of the list, that's all.'

Bankier admitted that he and the others had failed to pick up blue stamps for their identity cards. 'How could you be so stupid?' shouted Oskar. He was not so upset with his workers, but the whole scene at the train station had made him feel sick and angry.

◆

By June of 1942 no one knew who to trust either inside or outside the ghetto. Children stopped talking if they heard a noise on the stairs; adults woke up from bad dreams and saw that they were living in a worse one. Fierce rumours met them in their rooms, on the street, on the factory floor: children were being taken off to be shot, or drowned, or operated on; old people were closed up in abandoned salt mines. Perhaps they believed they could prevent the rumours from becoming true if they spoke them out loud. That June, unfortunately, the worst rumour became a fact, and Oskar and Ingrid were witnesses.

The handsome German lovers hired horses early one summer morning and rode off into the hills above the city. They stopped after a good ride and looked down into the ghetto. At first they were confused by what they saw, but soon they began to understand. A group of SS men, working with dogs, were going from house to house and forcing everyone out into the street.

Oskar noticed that two lines kept forming in Wegierska Street: one, with healthy-looking adults, did not move; the other, with the old, the very young and the weak, was regularly marched away into another street and moved out of sight. Families were divided and could do nothing about it; Oskar understood what this meant.

The couple on horses moved on to a place where they could see a different street. They watched as a line made up of a few women and many more children was led towards the train station. They noticed a slow-moving little child dressed in a small red coat and cap at the end of the line. The bright colour caught Oskar's eye; it made a statement about the child's love for red, but also about an individual life. A young SS man kept the little girl in line with the others with an occasional gentle touch on her arm. Oskar and Ingrid felt a brief sense of relief, thinking that these children would be treated kindly, but it did not last long.

They became aware of terrible noises from the surrounding streets. The SS teams with dogs were now going through every building a second time and chasing on to the pavement the men, women and children who had hidden in basements or cupboards, inside wardrobes or behind walls during the first search. As they reached the street, screaming and crying in terror of the dogs and guns, they were shot and left there. Schindler could see a mother and her thin son, perhaps eight years old, hiding behind some rubbish bins. He felt an uncontrollable fear for them and saw that Ingrid had seen them too, and was crying beside him.

With a terrible sense of alarm Oskar searched the streets for little Redcap. When his eyes found her, he realized that she and the others in her line could see the murders taking place on the next street. The horror of these actions was made much worse because witnesses had been permitted. Redcap stopped and turned to watch as the SS men shot the woman behind the bin, and one of the men, when the boy fell to the ground crying, put his boot down on the child's head and shot him in the back of the neck.

Little Redcap stared, but the kindly SS guard moved her forward again. Oskar could not understand this gentleness, since he, and somehow even the child, knew that mercy had been cancelled on the next street. If they permitted witnesses, those witnesses would not survive. Oskar knew that this scene would be happening over and over again throughout the German territories, carried out by SS men with official orders from the Nazi government.

More than 7,000 people were cleared from the ghetto during that weekend in June, and at the Gestapo office the *Aktion* was declared a great success. Oskar later remembered his own feelings and told people: 'Beyond this day, no thinking person could fail to see what would happen. I decided at that moment to do everything in my power to defeat the system.'

Chapter 5 Krakow's Jews Are Not Alone

Oskar Schindler did not keep a written account of Nazi crimes, but he began to notice more and to listen to more stories of what was happening. He wanted solid evidence that would allow him to make an accurate report to the world one day. He got news from police contacts, but also from clear-thinking Jews like Itzhak Stern and from organizations which either officially or secretly were working against the Nazis. Wild rumours flew through the streets of Krakow, but for a long time the people of the ghetto chose to ignore them and continued to hope. Realization for the ghetto began with the return to Krakow, eight days after he had been sent to one of the concentration camps, of a young chemist named Bachner.

Bachner returned to the ghetto with white hair and madness in his eyes. He had seen the final horror in Belzec, a death camp, and told his story to everyone he met. At the camp, SS men pushed the crowds of Jews along to two large buildings, where they were made to undress. A young boy moved among them, giving them string with which to tie their shoes together and collecting their rings and glasses. Then the prisoners had their heads shaved before being led to different buildings, each of which had a Jewish star on the roof and a sign which said 'Baths and Disinfection Rooms'. SS men encouraged them all the way, telling them to breathe deeply inside the building because it was an excellent means of preventing disease.

In the buildings, said Bachner, they were all gassed, and afterwards teams of SS men sorted out the terrible, twisted piles of bodies and moved them away to be buried. Only two days after they left Krakow station, they were all dead, except for Bachner. The calm tone of the SS men had alarmed him, and he had somehow slipped away to a toilet hut. He had hidden inside a toilet pit and stayed there for three days, with human waste up to his neck. He had feared drowning but had found a way to lean against the corner of the hole and sleep. On the third night he had crawled out and escaped. Outside the camp, a peasant woman cleaned him and put him into fresh clothes before he walked back to Krakow.

Maybe Bachner was completely mad, but his story fitted with what Schindler knew. The huge gas chambers of Belzec had been completed several months ago by a German engineering firm; 3,000 killings a day were possible there. Crematoria were under construction throughout the German territories. Oskar heard the names Sobibor, Lublin, Treblinka, Auschwitz, Lódz, Chelmno; all of these camps had gas chambers with the new technology. He heard that at one of the Auschwitz camps 10,000 people could be murdered in one day.

Oskar, and others who felt like him about the Nazis' actions against the Jews, began to put their own lives at risk. Oskar started to build barracks for his night workers behind DEF. When there was an *Aktion*, which by October was almost daily, workers from his factory, as well as from other factories, found shelter there and had the excuse of being at work in an essential industry. Other sympathetic Germans smuggled Jewish children out of the ghetto in boxes or provided families with false documents to get them out. A Jewish organization of young people, which worked to save Jewish lives, fought its own war against the Nazis. They secretly attacked small German boats; they disguised themselves in SS uniforms and planted bombs in restaurants, cinemas and military garages throughout the city; they made non-Jewish passports for people in the ghetto, and risked their own lives every day.

By the autumn of 1942 Jews in other parts of the world began to hear rumours of what was happening in the German territories. They wanted more information, and then a way to help. One of these people was a Budapest jeweller called Samu Springmann who began working with Jews in Istanbul to get rescue money into the German territories and to get accurate information out. He found Dr Sedlacek, an Austrian dentist who could travel freely in and out of Poland, and sent him to Krakow at the end of 1942 with a piece of paper in his pocket. It was a list of people that Jews in Palestine had learnt – probably from men like Itzhak Stern – were honourable people. The second name on the list was *Oskar Schindler*.

On his first evening in Krakow Dr Sedlacek met with Major Franz von Korab, a German officer and an old friend from their student days in Vienna, at the Hotel Krakovia. Once, a long time ago and against all good sense, but for the sake of friendship, von Korab had confessed to Sedlacek that he had a Jewish grandmother. Knowing this secret and keeping it safe meant that the dentist could trust von Korab with secret information that he now carried with him: he showed the German military officer the list from the Palestinian Jews.

Von Korab looked over the list and pointed to *Oskar Schindler*. 'I know Herr Schindler very well,' he laughed. 'I've dined with him many times. He's a big man, with an enormous appetite for life. He's making a lot of money from this war and spending a lot too. Very clever – more intelligent than he pretends to be. I can phone him now and arrange a meeting.'

At ten the next morning, after polite introductions had been made, von Korab left Dr Sedlacek in the director's office at DEF.

After explaining the purpose of his trip, the dentist asked, 'What can you tell us about the war against the Jews in Poland?'

Oskar hesitated and Sedlacek wondered if he was willing to risk his success, even his life, in order to help a few Jews. Schindler's factory now employed over 550 Jews, for which he paid the SS a slave wage, and he had rich military contracts from the German government and the guarantee of many more. Most men in his position would simply lean back in their comfortable chairs and claim not to know what people like Sedlacek were talking about, but Oskar surprised the dentist.

'There is one problem,' Oskar whispered roughly. 'It's this: what they are doing to people in this country is beyond belief.'

Sedlacek was shocked to hear the details of the official extinction of a whole race of people. The story that Schindler told him was not only terrible in moral terms but was hard to believe in the middle of a desperate war. The Nazis were using thousands of men, precious resources and expensive engineering and scientific technology to murder a race of people, not for military or economic gain, but for a psychological victory.

'The Nazis are closing the ghettos, in Krakow as well as in Warsaw and Lódz. The population of the Krakow ghetto has already been reduced by four-fifths,' said Schindler.

'What have they done with those people?' asked the dentist.

'Some were sent to labour camps. In the past few weeks, about 2,000 ghetto workers from Krakow have been marched every day to a site near the city to build a vast labour camp at the village of Plaszów. The labour camps don't have crematoria, so the Jews who are sent there can expect to be used as slave labour. But at least three-fifths of the Jews from the Krakow ghetto were transported to camps that have the new scientific equipment. These camps are common now; they are death camps.'

'How can you be sure?' asked Sedlacek.

'I know where the crematoria have been built; I know where the trains full of Jews have gone. I hear and see too much every day. Shall I tell you another little story about four jewellers?'

'Yes, of course,' answered the dentist. It was painful to hear what Schindler had to say, but he needed as much real information as possible to take back to Samu Springmann.

'One morning recently,' Schindler began, 'an SS man arrived at the Krakow ghetto and took away four men, all of whom had been jewellers by profession. They felt a sense of relief when the SS officer marched them past the train station to the old Technical College, which is now used for the SS Economic and Administration Office.

'The jewellers were led into the huge basement and saw walls piled high with suitcases and trunks, each with the name of the former owner carefully written on the side. And do you have any idea what their job was?'

'No, I can't imagine,' said Sedlacek quietly.

'They spent six weeks going through the gold and silver, the diamonds and pearls that came out of those suitcases. They weighed and valued each piece and put it into the correct box, and as each box was filled and labelled, it was sent to Nazi headquarters in Berlin.

'They acted professionally and could sometimes forget about

where all the stuff had come from until they were given suitcases full of gold teeth, still marked with blood. After valuing hundreds of thousands of teeth, would you still have any hope?'

At the end of this shocking meeting, an exhausted Sedlacek asked Schindler if he would come to Budapest to tell others what he had just reported to him. Oskar Schindler visited Budapest that December to give Springmann and his colleagues the first eye-witness account of the Polish horror. His report changed these men forever. They promised to get the information to Jews in Istanbul and Palestine, as well as to the governments of Great Britain and the United States.

Chapter 6 Amon Goeth Closes Krakow's Ghetto

In February 1943, as Oskar Schindler returned by train from Budapest, where he had predicted that the Krakow ghetto would soon be closed, another young German was on his way to Krakow with orders to do exactly that job. Commandant Amon Goeth and Oskar Schindler could in some ways be described as twins, with Goeth being the evil one. He had been born in the same year as Oskar, had been raised as a Catholic and had studied engineering at secondary school. Like Oskar, Amon Goeth was a huge, tall man with a weakness for good food, alcohol, splendid clothes and sex, but his sexual habits were not what everyone would describe as 'normal'. He was often very romantic at the beginning of a relationship, but then beat women when he became bored or angry with them.

He had been a Nazi since 1930, and after 1940 had risen quickly in the SS. He had been in charge of special teams of soldiers during *Aktions* in the crowded ghettos of Lublin and, because of his excellent performance there, had earned the right to destroy the Krakow ghetto. He was excited about this opportunity and knew it was important for his career, so he was determined to concentrate on the job, even though he had not been sleeping well and had been drinking more than ever recently. But he would do the job – he would clear the ghetto within a month of the date of his orders – and then he would be in charge of the labour camp that was being built at Plaszów.

Commandant Goeth was met in Krakow by two SS officers and taken directly to the ghetto. 'The ghetto is divided into two sections,' explained Horst Pilarzik, one of the young officers. 'On the left is Ghetto B with about 2,000 inhabitants who escaped earlier *Aktions* but who are not useful to us. They do not have appropriate skills and have not been given new identification cards. We'll ship them out of Krakow to Auschwitz immediately.

'On the other side you'll see Ghetto A, which still contains more than 10,000 people. They will be transferred to Plaszów and become the first labour force there. We plan to move the most important factories, which are owned by Germans of course, into the camp, so we will no longer have to march the Jews to and from their work every day.'

The small group moved out of the city to have a look at the progress being made on the camp at Plaszów. There was still a lot to be done, but with modern methods and plenty of free labour, these places could be built almost overnight. Amon Goeth was satisfied and excited by what he saw and looked forward to his meeting at Police Chief Scherner's office the next day to talk to the local factory owners. Privately he was calculating how much money he could make from the work that would go on in *his* camp. He had reached that happy point in his career at which duty and financial opportunity come together.

Goeth walked through the camp and came to the SS apartments where the work was under the direction of an excellent officer called Albert Hujar. Hujar marched up and made his report to the new commandant: 'Sir, a section of this building has fallen down.'

While Hujar was talking, Goeth noticed a girl walking around the half-finished building, shouting at the teams of men.

'Who is that?' Goeth asked Hujar.

'She is a prisoner, sir, named Diana Reiter. She's an architect and an engineer, in charge of constructing the housing for the camp. She says that the basement of this building was not dug properly and that we must tear it down and begin again.'

Goeth could tell that Hujar had been arguing with this woman. He smiled at the SS officer and said, 'We're not going to argue with these people. Get the girl.'

Diana Reiter walked towards Commandant Goeth; he judged her as he watched how she moved and how she held her head. To him she was the sort of Jew that he hated most: the type that still thought they were important.

'You have argued with Officer Hujar,' Goeth said.

'Yes, sir,' the girl said confidently. 'The basement at the north end must be re-dug or the whole building will fall down.' She went on arguing her case intelligently, as if she was talking to a fellow engineer. The commandant nodded but knew that you could never believe anything a Jew, especially a Jewish specialist, tried to tell you. Her attitude of authority was an insult to him.

'Hujar!' Amon Goeth shouted suddenly. The SS officer returned, thinking he was going to be told to follow the girl's orders. The girl did too, because she knew she was right.

'Shoot her,' Goeth told Hujar. The younger man paused and looked closely at the commandant. 'Shoot her now,' Goeth repeated. 'Here, on my authority.'

Hujar knew how it was done. He pushed the young architect forward, took out his gun and shot her in the back of the neck. Everyone in the camp stopped for a second but then quickly went back to work. Diana Reiter looked at Amon Goeth before she died with a look that frightened but also excited him. He believed that political, racial and moral justice had been done.

But later that evening the new commandant would suffer for this act and have an empty feeling that he tried to cure with food, alcohol and contact with a woman.

Next morning Goeth ignored any feelings of guilt he might have had the night before. The Jewish workers would never be lazy or difficult with him in charge; they had learnt what could happen in this camp. Hujar and his colleagues knew that quick judgement, followed by immediate murder, was the permitted style at Plaszów.

Later that morning as he sat in Police Chief Scherner's office and listened to him speaking to Oskar Schindler and the other factory owners, Goeth felt full of confidence. 'We'll do everything we can to make this camp work for you: your labour on site, no rent and no charges for maintaining the buildings.'

Goeth stood up and added, 'We are pleased to be partners with businessmen who have already made very valuable contributions to the war effort. I will not get in the way of the smooth operation of your businesses, and I will offer you as much help as possible inside the camp: housing for the workers, as well as for the SS guards and administrative staff, watch towers, good roads, a railway link and buildings with cement floors for industrial occupation. I hope that all of you will move your factories inside the camp walls as soon as possible.'

Two days later, after hearing the news of the murder of Diana Reiter, Oskar Schindler arrived at Commandant Goeth's office with a bottle of whisky under his arm. Schindler knew that he had to pretend to agree with everything Goeth said and did, but he was determined to keep his factory outside Plaszów.

The two big men sat opposite each other and understood what they had in common: they were both in Krakow to make a fortune and each of them had his own way of working within an evil system – one fought against it and the other pushed it to its extreme limit. Oskar turned on his salesman's charm and by listing his reasons for keeping DEF outside the camp – all of which had to do with being able to meet the demands of his military contracts – he persuaded Goeth to allow the factory to stay at its original site. His workers would stay at Plaszów and march to and from work each day. Oskar had made Goeth think that he was granting a favour for a friend, although he would always hate the commandant and everything he represented.

'I am very grateful for this decision, Herr Commandant,' said Oskar, 'and I'm sure our army will also be grateful.'

Amon Goeth knew this meant regular gifts from his new 'friend': drink, diamonds, women, even enamelware.

◆

On the ghetto's last morning, 13 March 1943, Amon Goeth and his team arrived at the main square an hour before dawn. The commandant drank from his bottle of whisky because, as usual, he was suffering from a morning headache due to lack of sleep. Now that he was here, though, he felt a certain professional excitement. Today was history. For more than seven centuries there had been a Jewish Krakow, and by tomorrow those 700 years would be no more than a rumour; Krakow would be free of Jews. Every minor SS official wanted to be able to say that he had seen it happen, and Goeth was thrilled to be leading this historic operation. He was not like some commandants who left the action to their men. He would show the way, as he had with Diana Reiter. He knew that when he was old and there were no Jews in the German empire, the young would ask him about this day.

It was a slow, tense day for Leopold Pfefferberg and Mila, the young wife he had married in the first days of the ghetto. They both had the blue stamp, but Leopold wanted to try to escape from the ghetto; he did not want to go to the labour camp at Plaszów. Mila, though, was afraid of her husband's proposed route out of the ghetto through the large underground waste pipes.

She had heard rumours that the SS would fill these pipes with gas and kill anyone who tried to escape through them. How could they decide to leave their little room and take this chance? And when?

Finally at midday, as they ate their ration of bread and listened to the terrible noise from the *Aktion* outside, Pfefferberg announced that he would go outdoors and see what was happening.

'Please don't leave me, Leopold,' begged Mila. 'You are all I have in this world.' Everyone in both their families was already dead – most of them murdered by the Nazis.

'I'll keep off the streets and go through the holes that connect the buildings,' her husband said calmly. 'I'll go to the doctor's house and find out if the pipes are still safe. I'll be back in five minutes. Just stay here and don't worry.'

Pfefferberg travelled quickly through the ghetto, keeping out of sight until he reached the Labour Office. Then he risked crossing the street and reached the doctor's building, but in the yard an old man told him that the doctor and his wife had left through the underground waste system.

Back home, Pfefferberg found that Mila and all their neighbours were gone, all the doors were opened, all the rooms were empty. He ran back outside, and on the pavement outside the hospital he saw a pile of about seventy dead bodies. These victims were people who had been marched here during the day and then shot. Pfefferberg recognized a few old clients of his mother's and parents of some of his students. Somehow he did not think of looking for Mila in this pile – instead, he raced on.

He found a crowd in Wegierska Street, loosely guarded by SS officers, and noticed some neighbours from his building. 'What has happened? Have you seen Mila?' he whispered.

'She'd already left when the SS arrived,' the neighbours said. 'She'll be near the gate by now, on her way to Plaszów.'

Pfefferberg decided to look for a good hiding place. He and Mila had said that if one of them was sent to Plaszów, the other one should try to stay out and get food to the one inside. Leopold hid behind the big iron gate near the Labour Office and watched the SS push people along. As they went through the gate, the Jews were forced to leave their suitcases behind on the ghetto street.

From his hiding place, Leopold could see three SS men and two large police dogs coming towards the gate. The dogs pulled one of the men into the building across the street while the other two waited on the pavement. One of the dogs dragged a screaming woman and her small child out of the building. The SS man pulled the child from its mother's arms and threw it against the brick wall, then he shot them both.

Perhaps before the woman and child were even dead, certainly before he had time to think, Leopold Pfefferberg stepped out into the street. He knew the dogs would find him, so instead of hiding, he began lifting suitcases and piling them against the walls of the yard. When the three men finally noticed him, Pfefferberg stood to attention, clapped his heels together like a good Polish soldier and addressed the tallest, most important-looking SS man.

'Herr Commandant!' he almost shouted. 'I respectfully report to you that I received an order to keep this road clear of all luggage.'

The dogs were pulling towards Pfefferberg, expecting to be told to kill this Jew, but instead of giving the order to kill, the commandant, with blood on his boots and trousers, smiled. Commandant Goeth was pleased to see a victim who could amuse him, and he threw back his head and laughed.

'We don't need you here,' Goeth said. 'The last group is leaving the ghetto. Now, get lost!'

Pfefferberg began to run, not looking back, and it would not have surprised him to get a bullet in his back as he joined a group of Jews at the main gate. He was in the last group that left the ghetto alive, but as they left they heard the nearly constant sound of gunfire. It meant that Amon Goeth and his team were bursting into basements, breaking down false ceilings, opening wooden boxes and finding people who all day had maintained a hopeful silence. More than 4,000 such people were discovered, pulled into the street and killed.

Chapter 7   Schindler's Double Life

On one of the first mornings at Plaszów, Commandant Goeth stepped out of his front door in his riding clothes and fine white shirt, carrying binoculars in one hand and his hunting gun in the other. He looked through the binoculars at the prisoners around the camp. In a relaxed manner, with a cigarette at the corner of his mouth, he took aim and for no apparent reason shot one of the prisoners. Goeth had chosen his target out of a group who were pushing and pulling carts of rocks to one of the building sites. The victim's body was thrown across the road when the bullet hit. The other workers stopped pushing, their muscles tensed, waiting for more bullets, but Amon Goeth waved them on; he was finished with them for the moment. This kind of unexpected shooting became a habitual part of the commandant's morning routine, reminding the prisoners that they would never know when it was their turn to die.

Such killing was just sport to Goeth and his SS men, but they also believed that it was their duty to murder Jews in order to make room at Plaszów for new prisoners as they arrived from different parts of the German territories. Sometimes the population at Plaszów rose to over 35,000 and the commandant had to find ways to control it. His quick method was to enter one of the camp workshops, order the prisoners to form two lines, and march one of them away. The prisoners in this line would either be taken to a hill behind the camp and shot immediately, or taken to the boxcars at Krakow Plaszów railway station and sent to the gas chambers in one of the death camps.

With his workers living at Plaszów, Oskar Schindler heard about what was going on in Goeth's evil empire. Apart from his extreme solutions to the growing numbers at the camp, Goeth also angered Schindler by breaking his promise that he would do nothing to stop the smooth running of the local factories. One day Oskar had a telephone call from Julian Madritsch, owner of the Madritsch Uniform Factory inside the camp, and one of the few other German owners who was trying to keep his 4,000 Jewish workers out of the death camps.

'Have you had any trouble with your workers arriving at DEF on time?' Madritsch asked.

'Yes, almost every day,' answered Schindler. 'Do you know what's going on?'

'It's Goeth's little games,' Madritsch said. 'Yesterday he found a potato hidden in one of the barracks, so every man from that barracks had to be publicly whipped in front of thousands of other prisoners with Commandant Goeth watching. My workers arrived several hours late, still shaking and unable to work properly.'

'There is a solution,' said Oskar. 'I'm thinking of keeping my workers at my factory site, away from Goeth's whips and guns.'

'Where would you put them? You don't have the space.'

'Not at the moment, but I think I know how to get more land.'

Oskar immediately began his efforts to build his own sub-camp beside DEF. He paid a very fair price to an elderly Polish couple for the land attached to the back of his factory and then went to see Amon Goeth and explained his plan for a sub-camp of Plaszów to be built in his own factory yard. This meant that Oskar would remove a significant number of Jews from Plaszów, perhaps as many as 2,000, and Goeth could make him pay for the new camp as well as for the continued care of the DEF workers. The commandant thought Oskar was a good fellow who was sick with a form of Jew-love, and he did not mind making a profit from his friend's illness.

Oskar followed the basic requirements for an SS Forced Labour Sub-camp by building three-metre fences, watchtowers, toilet huts, barracks, medical buildings, a bath house, a food store, a laundry and offices. That year DEF made a fortune for Schindler, but he also spent a small fortune on building his sub-camp, and he was only just beginning to pay for the privilege of saving Jewish lives.

When news began to spread that Herr Schindler was building his own camp, competition for a place there became fierce. People who got into the new camp would later recall it as a kind of heaven; they were contrasting it with Plaszów of course, but certainly it was a place where people had hope and a sense of safety. The guards were changed every two days, and they looked forward to their time at DEF because the food was better, Herr Schindler was generous with his whisky and they were not allowed inside the factory; their job was boring, but easy.

Inside Schindler's camp there were no dogs and no beatings. There was more and better soup and bread than at Plaszów, and even though the prisoners worked long hours – Oskar was still a businessman with war contracts to fill and a desire for profit – the work was reasonable. At DEF no one died from overwork, beatings or hunger, whereas at I G Farben's plant, a typical German factory with workers from Plaszów, 25,000 prisoners out of a work force of 35,000 would die at their labour.

◆

Itzhak Stern, now working in the Plaszów administration office, wanted to get Manasha Levartov, a young intellectual rabbi, into

Oskar's sub-camp. Stern admired Levartov for his understanding of Jewish law and history and worried that Goeth would make him a target because he was too intelligent and too well-educated.

On a morning when Plaszów held over 30,000 prisoners, the commandant decided to reduce the numbers in the metalworks factory, and Levartov found himself in what seemed to be the safe line. Suddenly a boy of about sixteen, who had a good idea of where his line was going, called out, 'But Herr Commandant, I'm a very good metalworker too.'

'Yes, child?' said Goeth softly. Then he took out his gun and shot the boy in the head. The rest of the men in the line were marched to the train and moved to a death camp. Levartov was sure that the commandant had noticed him and believed he had avoided a bullet from his gun only because the young boy had dared to speak; he would not be safe for long.

Within a few days Goeth returned to the metalworks and began to select prisoners to be taken to the hill to be shot. He stopped beside Rabbi Levartov and asked, 'What are you making?'

'Herr Commandant,' said Levartov, 'I am making machine hinges.' He pointed to the small heap of metal hinges on the floor.

'Make me one now,' ordered Goeth. He looked at his watch and began timing the rabbi. Levartov cut a hinge and put it together as quickly as his nervous fingers would move.

'Another,' the commandant ordered as soon as the rabbi had finished the first one.

After the second metal hinge was completed, Goeth, without raising his eyes from the pile of finished work on the floor, said, 'You've been working here since six this morning and can make a metal hinge in less than one minute, but you have only made this ridiculous little pile of hinges.'

Goeth led the rabbi outside and stood him against the workshop wall. Then he took out his gun, the same one he had used to shoot the sixteen-year-old boy, held it to Levartov's head and fired, but nothing happened. Goeth opened his gun, checked the bullets, returned it to Rabbi Levartov's head and fired again – but still nothing happened.

The commandant began cursing wildly before taking a smaller gun from his jacket pocket. Rabbi Levartov knew that Goeth would not be stopped by a technical problem. He began praying again, and waited for the gun at his head to fire, but again the gun failed to go off.

Now Levartov decided to speak. 'Herr Commandant, I beg to report that I had only a small pile of hinges beside me today because I was sent to carry coal this morning.'

Red with anger, Goeth hit the rabbi across the face and stormed away, leaving Levartov against the wall with a bleeding mouth. However, he knew the battle had only come to a temporary stop.

Itzhak Stern reported this incident to Oskar Schindler in the Building Office at Plaszów. When Stern finished, Oskar said, 'Why the long story? There's always room at DEF for someone who can make a metal hinge in less than a minute.'

Levartov and his wife moved to the DEF camp in the summer of 1943, and at first the rabbi thought Schindler was making cruel jokes on Friday afternoons when he said, 'You shouldn't be here, Rabbi. You should be preparing for holy services.'

But when Oskar gave Levartov a bottle of wine for use in the Friday night Jewish ceremonies, the rabbi knew that the Herr Director was not joking. From that day Levartov was allowed to leave his workbench before the sun went down on Friday afternoons, return to his prisoners' barracks and do his duty as a rabbi by performing a holy Jewish ceremony.

◆

When he was settled in Plaszów, Amon Goeth began to give grand parties, and Oskar Schindler was one of his favourite guests. As much as he enjoyed good food and wine and the company of attractive women, Oskar hated receiving an invitation to a social event from Commandant Goeth. There had, in fact, never been a time when sitting at Goeth's table had not been a disturbing business, but by the autumn of 1943 Oskar found the idea disgusting.

As he and his driver approached the gates of the labour camp, Oskar, with an expensive gift in his pocket for Goeth, prepared himself to act the sociable role that was expected of him. He would be a sympathetic listener when Goeth complained about the Jews or told a joke or sang a song. He would charm the female guests – usually women who were paid to keep the gentlemen guests happy – and would promise boxes of enamelware to various German officials, all the time smiling and looking for the first opportunity to escape. The idea of getting drunk or having sex at Goeth's house did not appeal to Schindler, and he felt a sense of relief when the commandant finally went upstairs with one of the pretty girls who had been hired to satisfy his wishes.

Oskar quickly said good night and left the other guests. In the hall, he saw Helen Hirsch, Goeth's Jewish housekeeper. He and everyone else had noticed this young woman as she served at the dining table because of the dark bruises along her jaw and even darker, almost purple, marks on her thin neck. Oskar had been surprised at dinner by the way Goeth had displayed the girl to the guests, rather than hiding her and her bruises in the kitchen.

The girl servant noticed Oskar and stood at attention, waiting for him to order her to do something.

'Please, Helen,' said Herr Schindler, 'you don't have to be afraid of me. Please, show me your kitchen.'

Helen Hirsch was afraid, but she knew she had no choice in these situations. The commandant's guests could order her to do what they wanted. In the kitchen Oskar asked, like a famous football player or actor, 'Don't you know me? I'm Schindler.'

With relief the girl said, 'Herr Director, of course, I've heard . . . And you've been here before. I remember . . .'

He put his arm around her and touched her cheek with his lips. He whispered, 'Don't worry, Helen, it's not that kind of kiss. I pity you for what you have to bear in this house.'

Helen Hirsch began to cry because of Schindler's kind words, and she saw that he was crying too. Then he stood back and looked at her. 'Itzhak Stern told me about you. No one should have to live like you do.'

'I've accepted my life,' said Helen. 'One day he'll shoot me. I've seen too many things.'

'He enjoys you too much to kill you. It's not decent, but it's life. If you can keep your health, you can hold on to your life.'

'But he'll kill me in the end,' said Helen quietly.

'I have a factory – surely you have heard of it?' asked Schindler.

'Oh yes,' the girl said like a starving child talking about a palace. 'Schindler's DEF. I've heard of it.'

'Keep your health. I'll try to get you out of here.'

In this crazy world at war Oskar had become like a character from a story, an almost imaginary figure: the good German. By this time in 1943, he had broken Reich laws to such an extent that he had earned a hundred bullets for his own head or a trip to Auschwitz. But he would not change his ways now; he would continue to spend his money and use his influence to save people like Helen Hirsch.

Chapter 8   Saint Oskar?

The Oskar Schindler who looked and dressed like a film star, went to elegant dinner parties and continued to make an enormous amount of money from his wartime factory was also the Oskar Schindler whose main concern was thinking of ways to save his Jews. How could he fit more prisoners into the DEF sub-camp? How could he find enough food for his camp kitchen? In 1943 he was one of a very small number of people in the whole of Poland who were willing to risk their lives to feed and protect 'the enemy'. By contrast, in the great death camps and the forced-labour camps, large and small, it was part of the official programme to starve the Jews to extinction.

Schindler also attempted to stop the murder of as many individuals as possible. He was away from Krakow on business when two brothers named Danziger accidentally cracked a metal press at DEF, and a factory spy reported the incident to the SS guards outside. The next morning the prisoners heard over the loudspeaker: *Tonight the people of Plaszów will witness the hanging of two criminals.*

Oskar returned from his trip three hours before the advertised hanging and drove immediately to Plaszów, taking several bottles of excellent wine and some fine Polish sausage. No one knows what kind of deal Schindler made with Commandant Goeth, but when he left Plaszów at six o'clock, the Danziger brothers were sitting in the back seat of his luxury car and were thrilled to be returning to the security of the DEF sub-camp.

Unfortunately Schindler was able to save very few of the Jews at Plaszów: ninety per cent of them did not survive to see the end of the war. It was a place where murder was especially frightening because it became such an ordinary, everyday occurrence. For the fraction of the Plaszów prisoners who did live on into the peace, the hanging of Emil Krautwirt was the first story they told after relating their own personal histories of their time in the camp.

This young engineer had received his diploma in the late 1930s and worked for Schindler at DEF. He was going to be hanged because of some letters he had written to people in Krakow. A sixteen-year-old boy, who had been heard singing Russian folk songs, would be hanged beside him. The prisoners stood in lines and listened as the young boy begged for his life.

'Herr Commandant,' the boy began in a shaking voice, 'I am not a Russian supporter. They were just ordinary school songs.'

The hangman placed the rope around the boy's neck. He could see that Goeth was losing patience with the boy's tragic begging. When the hangman kicked the support from beneath the boy's feet, the rope broke and the boy, purple and almost unable to breathe, with the rope still around his neck, crawled on his hands and knees to Goeth. He begged to be allowed to live, hitting his head against the commandant's ankles and holding on to his legs. It was a terrible act of surrender, and it emphasized Goeth's kingly position. Surrounded by total silence, the commandant kicked the boy away and shot him through the head.

When the engineer saw the boy's horrible death, he took a razor blade he had hidden in his pocket and cut his wrists. In spite of this, Goeth ordered the hangman to proceed with his job, and the Jews of southern Poland, including children, were forced to watch as Krautwirt was hanged with blood pouring from his wrists.

Even while such terrible events were happening very close to him, Schindler continued to search for more ways to help the Jews. Dr Sedlacek returned from Austria to Krakow in 1943, and Oskar persuaded Itzhak Stern, who was not sure he should trust Sedlacek, to write a full account of the situation at Plaszów for the dentist to take back to rescue organizations in Budapest and Istanbul. In the end Stern wrote a clear and honest report that told the story of what was happening at Plaszów, as well as at the other 1,700 labour camps, large and small, in Poland. It was a report that would shock the world.

At the same time that Schindler was protecting his Jews and Itzhak Stern was writing reports, another German Catholic, Raimund Titsch, the manager of Madritsch's uniform factory, was saving lives by playing chess with the commandant. The first time they had played, Goeth had lost within half an hour and marched angrily out of his living room. Titsch had worried that the commandant was going out to find a Jew to punish for his defeat. Since that afternoon Titsch had taken as long as three hours to lose to the commandant. Workers who saw him arrive at Goeth's house with his chess board now spread the word that the commandant was playing chess and everyone could expect a sane afternoon.

But Raimund Titsch did not only play preventative chess. He had secretly begun to photograph everything that happened at Plaszów. He made a permanent record of the cruel forced labour in the camp, in the factories and in a mine near the camp. He showed the condition of the starving prisoners, as well as where they lived, what they ate, where they died and were buried. He photographed the SS men and the Ukrainian guards marching, at work, at play. Some of his pictures showed the size of the camp and how empty and lonely it was with roads made from broken Jewish gravestones. Some even showed a fat Amon Goeth relaxing in the sun on his balcony with his two big, vicious dogs and his Polish lover, Majola.

As he finished each roll of film, Titsch hid it in a steel box in his Krakow apartment and never actually saw the photographs himself. Even after the war he was afraid of being called a 'Jew-lover' and of being punished for taking such photographs by a secret society of former SS men. The Plaszów rolls of film were not developed until after Titsch died in the 1960s, when Leopold Pfefferberg bought the film. Nearly all the pictures came out clearly.

◆

In the early days of 1944 the Plaszów Forced Labour Camp and Oskar's sub-camp became concentration camps, which meant that they were now under the authority of General Oswald Pohl and the SS Main Economic and Administration Office in Berlin, instead of being under the authority of the local German police chiefs. Fees for labour now had to be sent to Pohl's office and if Oskar wanted a favour or any information about the future of his camp, he had to talk to someone in Berlin as well as to Amon Goeth in Krakow. Oskar decided to go to Berlin to meet his new bosses and find out what they planned to do with DEF, a very small operation compared to some of the huge factories and camps that Pohl's office was also in charge of. A minor personnel officer was appointed to meet Herr Schindler.

'I hope you don't want to increase the size of your camp,' said the officer. 'It would be impossible to do so without an increased risk of spreading disease.'

Oskar dismissed this suggestion with a wave of his hand. 'I am interested in having a permanent labour force. I've discussed this matter with my friend, Colonel Erich Lange. I have a letter from him which explains the importance of my factory to the war effort. Both he and I hope that my work will not be stopped by moving my highly skilled workers from place to place.'

He could see that the personnel officer was impressed with the letter from Lange. The colonel was a man of influence at Army Headquarters in Berlin.

Oskar and Lange had met at a party in Krakow and had realized that they shared certain ideas about the Nazis' treatment of Jews. Lange had been shocked by the factory camps of Poland – by the Farben works at Buna, for example, where Jews worked until they dropped. Their dead bodies were then thrown into ditches and covered with cement.

'Herr Schindler,' the personnel officer continued, 'there are no plans to alter your factory or sub-camp, and we do not wish to move your workers. But you must understand that the situation of Jews, even in a company with military contracts, is always risky. Sometimes the SS officers away from Berlin make their own decisions. Even at the death camps, they sometimes forget to keep enough Jews alive to do the work in the camp. But I don't think you'll have any problems with your work force,' he finished, tapping the letter from Lange.

Oskar returned to Krakow with at least some guarantee that his factory and his Jews were safe for the moment.

Chapter 9 Schindler's List

Schindler's thirty-sixth birthday, 28 April 1944, was a quiet day without celebrations either in the office or on the factory floor, although Oskar did receive good wishes from his wife in Zwittau and gifts from both Ingrid and Victoria. Oskar was not in a party mood because he was upset about the war news. The Russian armies had come to a stop instead of continuing south into the German territories. Was he hoping for a German defeat without considering what that would mean to his factory and sub-camp?

At the same time the possibility that the Russians might reach Poland was making life more complicated for Amon Goeth. The Nazis did not want their enemies to find any evidence of what they were doing to the Jews, so the SS had been ordered to destroy the gas chambers and crematoria at many of the death camps. The huge camp at Auschwitz would finish the job, and then the Nazis planned to destroy that as well.

Plaszów had never had a gas chamber or crematorium, but its dead lay everywhere around it, and now Goeth was ordered to find and burn them. Estimates of the number of bodies at Plaszów vary widely, with some as high as 80,000. Most victims had been shot or hanged, or had died from disease. Oskar saw and smelled the piles of burning flesh and bones on the hill above the workshops during a visit to Plaszów just before his birthday. He walked into the Administration Office and found Itzhak

Stern. Instead of making his usual polite conversation, he whispered, 'Stern, what does everyone think?'

'Herr Schindler, prisoners are prisoners. They do their work and hope to survive to see another day.'

'I'm going to get you *all* out,' Oskar said as he banged on Stern's desk with his fist.

'All?' asked Itzhak Stern. He knew that such promises could not match the reality of the situation.

'You, anyhow,' said Oskar. '*You.*'

As he left Stern's office, Oskar was depressed to see the ordinary life of the camp going on as the air filled with the thick smoke and terrible smell of burning bodies.

◆

Of course many people began to wonder how long their 'ordinary' life in Plaszów could continue. One of these was Mietek Pemper, a studious young prisoner who worked in the Administration Office beside Amon Goeth's private secretary, a young German woman called Frau Kochmann. Pemper was not supposed to see any secret Nazi documents or to read any important orders from Nazi headquarters, but because he was a much more skilful secretary than Frau Kochmann, he eventually saw almost everything that came to the office. Besides being an expert typist, Pemper also had a photographic memory, and he stored the details of beatings, hangings and mass murders in his head, without needing to write any of the information down. He knew that this was his death sentence; he was a witness that Commandant Goeth would, in the end, have to get rid of.

At the end of April Pemper read a letter from Berlin that he would always remember. A labour chief was asking Goeth how many Hungarian Jewish prisoners could be held temporarily at Plaszów, while a weapons factory at Auschwitz prepared itself to receive them. The Labour Department would be very grateful if

Goeth could take as many as 7,000 of these recent, relatively healthy prisoners.

Goeth's answer, either seen or typed by Pemper, stated that there was no room at Plaszów, but he would be happy to accept 10,000 prisoners on their way to Auschwitz if he were given permission to get rid of the unproductive prisoners inside the camp. Goeth was later pleased to receive notice that the director of the gas chambers at Auschwitz-Birkenau would expect a group of unfit prisoners to be delivered from Plaszów, and that transport would be arranged from the gate of his camp.

With his orders in hand Amon Goeth confidently planned his sorting process, which he called the Health Action. In one horrible day he would sentence to death as many prisoners as Oskar Schindler was keeping safe at DEF.

The Health Action on Sunday 7 May was organized a bit like a county fair. The square was hung with signs that said: *To Every Prisoner, Appropriate Work!* Loudspeakers played popular music, and at a long table sat the eccentric Dr Blancke, Dr Leon Gross and a number of clerks. The SS doctors assessed the entire prison population by having the prisoners remove all their clothes and run up and down in front of the table. While the music played the doctors looked for signs of disease and injury, and the clerks recorded the names of the people the doctors judged to be too weak to work, including the children. The prisoners were running for their lives, with their stomachs turning and their lungs fighting for air.

Fortunately many of the camp children survived the Health Action by hiding on that terrible day. Several hid silently in the ceiling of a barracks, not moving to get food or water or to go to the toilet for hours. The guards avoided the ceilings because they believed the rats that lived up there carried disease.

One fairly tall thirteen-year-old orphan had usually passed as a man, but without his clothes it was obvious that he was still a child, so he was marked down to go to Auschwitz. The boy had to join the children who were leaving the camp, but after a few minutes he quietly moved away from the group and stood with the safe adults. After another minute or two, he held his stomach and asked a guard for permission to go to the toilet huts.

Arriving at the huts, the boy climbed into a toilet hole and found a place to put his feet on either side of the hole. The smell blinded him and flies crawled into his mouth, ears and nose. Then he thought he heard ghosts.

'Did they follow you?' whispered a young voice.

'This is our place! There isn't room for you,' said another.

There were ten children in there with him.

At the end of the process 1,402 adults and 68 children stood in the square, ready to be transferred to the gas chambers of Auschwitz. Goeth considered the figures disappointing, but they made enough room for Plaszów to receive quite a large number of Hungarian prisoners.

One hot afternoon, soon after the Health Action, Schindler and the other factory owners were called to a meeting at the commandant's office. Amon Goeth spent the entire time warning them that there were Poles in Warsaw who were planning to attack the camp and release the prisoners. Oskar knew that no such thing would ever happen and could tell that Amon Goeth had a secret motive in telling him and the other owners this ridiculous story, but he was not sure what it was.

After the meeting Oskar gave Goeth some beautiful, handmade leather riding equipment. Because the fees for his workers now went straight to Berlin, Oskar understood that regular gifts for Goeth were necessary to keep him friendly. As the two men drove through the camp to the commandant's house, they could see that the boxcars standing on the railway tracks were full of prisoners, and they could hear the sound of suffering from inside. Oskar stopped his car and listened. Goeth, who was feeling very happy with his gift, smiled at his emotional friend.

'Some of them are from Plaszów,' said Goeth, 'and some from the Montelupich prison. They're complaining now? They don't know what suffering is yet.'

The roofs of the boxcars were burning hot in the afternoon sun.

'Commandant, if you don't object, I'll call out your fire department,' Oskar said.

For some reason Goeth decided to sit back and watch what Schindler might do. When the firemen arrived, Oskar instructed them to turn the water on to the boxcars and cool them down. Then he opened the doors and passed buckets of water inside and had the prisoners pass out any dead bodies. Before the train left the station, he gave the driver a basket of cigarettes, wine, cheese and sausage, and asked him to open the doors when the train stopped near stations and to give the prisoners water.

Goeth was entertained by Oskar's performance, but he was also worried about him. Schindler's need to help the Jews had reached a new, passionate level and his actions were becoming more and more dangerous. After the train left, Goeth said, 'You have to relax, my friend. You can't go running after every train that leaves this place. You can't change their final destination.'

Others, including the prisoner Adam Garde, also noticed that Schindler's need to stop the madness going on around him became more and more desperate. On the night of 20 June an SS man came to Garde's barracks. 'Herr Schindler has called the guardhouse,' the man told Garde. 'It is necessary for you to go to his office immediately.'

Garde found Oskar listening to a German radio station with a bottle and two glasses on the table in front of him. He pointed to a chair and a glass of whisky for Garde as he concentrated on what the announcer was saying. Finally he turned to the young Jew and said, 'Someone has tried to kill Hitler. They announced it earlier this evening and then said that Hitler had survived and would soon speak to the German people, but that was hours ago, and they haven't produced him yet.'

'What do you think it means?' asked Garde.

'I think he might be dead,' said Oskar with hope rising in his voice. 'Just think, it could be the end of the SS, the end of people like Himmler and the death camps.' The ten o'clock news repeated the earlier story, but still Hitler did not speak.

'Our troubles are over,' Oskar said. 'The world is sane again. Germany can join the western powers and defeat the Russians.'

Garde began to hope that Oskar was right, but all he wished for was a safe place, even an old-fashioned ghetto, for the Polish Jews. The same message was repeated every hour as the two men sat together drinking whisky and hoping. But a little before one o'clock in the morning, Hitler began broadcasting from Rastenberg. 'My fellow Germans!' the voice began. 'I am unhurt and well.' The speech ended four minutes later with Hitler's promise to punish those who had tried to murder him.

Garde had never really believed that the world would be different in the morning, but Oskar had and now he was filled with grief. 'Our vision of liberation will have to wait,' he said, as if they were both prisoners waiting to be released. Garde was surprised to see how depressed Schindler now looked. Until lately he had always seemed so practical and optimistic.

◆

Later that summer Oskar found out the real purpose of Goeth's last meeting with the factory owners. The commandant had heard a rumour that Plaszów and the other labour camps would soon be closed, so he went to the SS police chief in Krakow and told him the story of a possible attack by Poles from Warsaw.

'If there's trouble at Plaszów,' Goeth said to the police chief, 'do I have your permission to shoot first and do the paperwork later?' Since General Pohl had been in charge of the camps, Goeth had not been allowed to kill prisoners without a genuine reason. If he ignored the rules from Berlin, he would get into trouble.

'No problem,' said the police chief, who was also unhappy with so many new orders from Berlin. 'If you're careful and use your judgement, I'll support you.'

Goeth now had an excuse to murder some of the prisoners at Plaszów who knew too much about him. Unfortunately for them, the whole Chilowicz family fell into this category. From the first days at Plaszów, they had made themselves useful to Goeth as his agents. They travelled between Plaszów and Krakow, doing business for the commandant: selling food that was meant for the prisoners, as well as jewellery and gold that had been found in the prisoners' clothes or hidden around the camp. They had enjoyed a privileged life, but Goeth believed that the Chilowiczes would try to trade information about him if they needed a way out of a death camp. A very fat Goeth, yellow with disease and having difficulty breathing by this time, had the whole family shot and then conveniently found a gun hidden in the father's boot; the gun was Goeth's proof that the Chilowiczes had been trying to escape from the camp.

When the bodies were displayed on the Plaszów square, they had signs tied around their chests which read: *Those who break fair laws can expect a similar death*. That, of course, was not the lesson the prisoners learnt from the sight.

The rumour that Amon Goeth had heard earlier in the summer was confirmed one morning when Oskar Schindler found orders from Army High Command waiting for him on his desk. Because of the war situation the concentration camp at Plaszów and the sub-camp beside DEF would close. Prisoners from DEF would be sent back to Plaszów to wait for the time when all the prisoners would be sent to another camp. Oskar's job, according to the orders, was to close his factory as quickly as possible.

Who were these people in Berlin who knew nothing about his Jews? Why didn't they name the camp that the prisoners would be moved to? At least, thought Oskar, people like General Frank, one of the top Nazis in Poland, had had the courage to tell the truth earlier in the year when he said in a speech, 'When we finally win this war, Poles, Ukrainians and all those prisoners idling about here can be cut up and made into dog food.' The bosses in Berlin wrote about 'another camp' and then believed they had no part in the final solution.

Goeth, on the other hand, knew exactly what 'another camp' meant and during Oskar's next visit he told him. 'All Plaszów men will be sent to Gröss-Rosen and will be worked to death in the vast mine in Lower Silesia. The women will go to Auschwitz, where the death machines are more direct and modern.'

When the news that DEF would be closed reached the factory floor and the sub-camp, many prisoners believed that they had reached the end of the road. They had had a few years of comparative rest, soup and sane treatment under Schindler, but they expected to die now. Rabbi Levartov feared facing Amon Goeth again. Edith Liebgold, who had been hired by Bankier for the night shift three years before, noticed that Herr Schindler no longer made promises of safety.

But at the end of the summer, when the DEF workers packed their bundles and were marched back to Plaszów, there was a rumour among them that Schindler had spoken of buying them back. Some refused to hope that the rumour could be true, but others began to believe that Schindler would get them out again; they began to believe that a *List* already existed, and surely their names were on it.

These Jews, it seems, knew Oskar Schindler very well because he began talking to Amon Goeth about taking Jews away from Krakow one night as the two men sat alone in Goeth's living room. The commandant was not hosting so many parties these days because Dr Blancke had warned him that if he did not eat and drink less, he would die.

Towards the end of a pleasant evening, Oskar began to talk more seriously. 'Commandant, I want to move my factory and my skilled workers to Czechoslovakia, near my home in Zwittau. I'll ask the appropriate office in Berlin for approval, and I'd be very grateful for any support you can give me.'

Goeth was always interested when Oskar talked about being 'grateful' and said, 'Yes, of course. If you can get Berlin to cooperate with your crazy scheme, I'll allow you to make a list of the workers you want from here.'

With business out of the way, Goeth wanted a game of cards. He knew that he would profit from helping Oskar with his plan, so now he did not mind risking some money on cards. They played a game that was not easy to lose on purpose and Oskar kept winning. Soon he had a pile of money in front of him, and Goeth called for Helen Hirsch to bring coffee. The servant came in, looking very clean and neat but with a swollen and bruised eye. Oskar observed to himself that she was so small that Goeth must have had to bend down to beat her.

It was almost a year since Oskar had promised to help Helen. He was always kind when she saw him at the house, but she could not let herself hope that she would escape from Goeth. Only a few weeks before, for example, when the soup was not the correct temperature, the commandant had called for two of his guards and told them to take Helen outside and shoot her.

As they marched her to a tree outside Goeth's window, Helen said to one of the men, 'Petr, who's this you're going to shoot? It's Helen who gives you cakes.'

'I know, Helen,' Petr whispered. 'I don't want to hurt you, but if I don't shoot you, he'll kill me and then you.'

Helen's legs were trembling violently as the men stood her against the tree. Then at the last moment they heard Goeth shouting, 'Bring her back. There's plenty of time to shoot her. Maybe I can still educate her.'

After their coffee, Oskar suggested a change in the betting. 'I'll need a housekeeper when I return to Czechoslovakia. It would be very difficult to find a servant as intelligent and well trained as Helen Hirsch. Let's play one more game and if you win, I'll pay you double the amount on the table. But if I win, then you give me Helen Hirsch for my list.'

'Let me think about that,' said Goeth.

'Come on,' encouraged Oskar. 'She's going to Auschwitz anyway.' Oskar tried to keep the tone of the conversation light, but he got up and found some official-looking paper and wrote: *By my authority the name of Helen Hirsch should be added to any list of skilled workers to be moved to Herr Oskar Schindler's factory in Zwittau.*

The card game did not last long, Oskar's luck continued and soon an angry Amon Goeth signed the paper Oskar had prepared. Out in her kitchen, Helen Hirsch had no idea that she had been saved over cards, but Schindler later talked about his evening with the commandant to Itzhak Stern, and soon rumours of Oskar's plan spread through Plaszów. There *was* a Schindler list, and it was worth everything to be on it.

Chapter 10 The Long Road to Safety

After the war Schindler's Jews would shake their heads and try to understand the complicated motives behind the Herr Director's willingness to risk his life to save them. Most of them said quite simply, 'I don't know why he did it.'

Others came to the conclusion that he enjoyed the games he had to play and the deals he had to make in order to keep them alive. Others said that he loved the satisfaction he felt in doing good, or that he was a rebel working against the evil he saw in the Nazi system. But none of these explanations could fully account for his fierce determination in the autumn of 1944 to find another safe place for the DEF workers.

Schindler's first step was to go to Berlin to talk to his friend Colonel Erich Lange at Army Headquarters. Lange could guarantee military contracts and strongly recommend to the Army High Command that Oskar be given permission to move his factory and workers to Zwittau. Lange wanted Oskar's plan to work, but he told him, 'We can do it, but it will take a lot of money. Not for me – for others.'

With Lange's support, Oskar was able to get approval from Berlin, but there were still problems. The governor of the Liberec area around Zwittau refused to allow any labour camps with Jewish prisoners in his district, and he had successfully kept such camps out throughout the war. Oskar was told to speak to an engineer in the Weapons Department named Sussmuth, and was reminded that if he wanted to get anything done, he should come to meetings with a good supply of sausage, top quality tobacco, wine, whisky and coffee. Oskar was used to this sort of thing, but by 1944 the price of such luxuries was extremely high. Nevertheless, Oskar continued spending.

In the middle of Oskar's trip to Berlin to see Sussmuth, Amon Goeth was arrested. Someone who was jealous of the commandant's very comfortable lifestyle had reported him, and now he was sitting in jail waiting for his trial, as senior SS investigators examined his finances. They did not care about the number of people Goeth had shot from his balcony or the number of Jews he had had killed on the hill behind his camp; they were more interested in his black market businesses and how he had treated some of his junior SS officers. They also searched the apartment Goeth kept in Krakow and found a large amount of cash, almost a million cigarettes and many other luxury items piled from floor to ceiling. He had obviously been using the flat as his private storehouse.

The investigators called in Helen Hirsch and Mietek Pemper,

but they were both sensible enough to keep their mouths shut. They knew what happened to prisoners who told the truth about their commandants: they were usually dead within hours of talking. They both wisely played the role of polite, blind servants, and soon the SS police took them back to Plaszów. Goeth's arrest had given these two a better chance at life, unless he was released too soon.

But Goeth was not released. His powerful friends did not step forward to help him, and the investigators were both shocked and envious at the way the commandant had been living.

Oskar was concerned about the investigations into Goeth's lifestyle and was worried that he would also be arrested or at least called in for questioning about his friendship with the former commandant. He was right to be worried because Goeth explained some of the cash in his Krakow apartment by saying, 'Oskar Schindler gave it to me to make life easier for his Jews.' But fortunately Oskar was not called in to answer questions about Amon Goeth at this time.

◆

To his surprise Oskar did not need the whisky and diamonds he took to his meeting with engineer Sussmuth, an honest and moral man. Oskar learnt that he had also proposed the idea of building some small Jewish work camps in the border towns between Poland and Czechoslovakia to make weapons for the German army. Even though these camps would be under the central control of either Auschwitz or Gröss-Rosen, Sussmuth knew that if the prisoners were in smaller camps, they would have a greater degree of safety. Unfortunately he had got nowhere with his plan because of objections from the local governor. Sussmuth did not have enough friends in high places to change the governor's mind, but perhaps Schindler, with the support of Colonel Lange and others, had the necessary influence.

'Herr Schindler,' said Sussmuth, 'I have investigated the border area and have made a list of suitable sites for small labour camps. There is one on the edge of Brinnlitz. Do you know this village?'

'Of course,' replied Schindler. 'It's very close to Zwittau, my home town. Which place are you talking about?'

'It's a cloth factory owned by the Hoffman brothers from Vienna. The business is very successful, but they have a very large building standing idle.'

'I know the factory you're talking about, and there's a local railway line from Zwittau to Brinnlitz,' said Oskar.

'Yes, I have that in my report,' said Sussmuth.

'But do you have in your report that my brother-in-law is in charge of the railway yard in Zwittau?'

'That's very good news,' said Sussmuth, smiling. 'I will write to Berlin and recommend the Hoffman building for your factory. With Colonel Lange behind you, I think you will succeed where I failed.'

Oskar left Sussmuth and drove to Brinnlitz to have a look at the Hoffman Brothers' Cloth Factory. He was able to walk into the empty building without being challenged and was delighted with what he found. There was enough space for his machines, his offices, his own apartment, and upstairs there was space for his Jews to live. He knew that the people of Brinnlitz would not be happy with the idea of more than a thousand Jews moving into their neighbourhood so late in the war. But after seeing this place Oskar was determined to spend whatever money was needed, to talk to the necessary people and to move his Jews to Brinnlitz.

A week after Oskar's meeting with Sussmuth the gentlemen of the appropriate Berlin office instructed the difficult governor in his castle in Liberec that Oskar Schindler's factory, with its military contracts and skilled workers, would be moving into the Hoffman brothers' empty building in Brinnlitz. The governor and other officials complained that a thousand Jews would bring disease and crime into the area; they said that Oskar's small factory would do very little to help the war effort but could make Brinnlitz a target for enemy bombs; they put signs up in the area which said: *Keep the Jewish Criminals Out*. But the protests had no effect because they had to go straight to Colonel Erich Lange's office in Berlin.

So with the help of Lange and Sussmuth, Oskar's plans went forward, but every step along the way was expensive. He had to pay to get permits, to get money moved from one bank account to another, to make friends in Brinnlitz. No one wanted cash, so Oskar had to search everywhere for tea, leather shoes, carpets, coffee, fish – whatever the people in charge wanted.

One of the people Oskar had to keep happy was Commandant Hassebroeck at Gröss-Rosen. Under Hassebroeck's management, 100,000 people died in the Gröss-Rosen system, but when Oskar talked to him he found him to be a type he had met before: a charming killer. Hassebroeck was excited about extending his empire further into Czechoslovakia. He already controlled 103 sub-camps and was pleased to be getting number 104.

Commandant Büscher, who had replaced Amon Goeth at Plaszów, knew about Schindler's list and told Oskar that it had to be completed and on his desk by a certain day. There were more than a thousand names on the dozen pages, which were the only papers in Plaszów with any connection to the future. The list included the names of all the prisoners of the sub-camp at DEF, as well as new names, including Helen Hirsch. Oskar had allowed Raimund Titsch to add names of prisoners from Madritsch's factory, but he had stopped him after seventy names because Berlin had set a limit of 1,100 for the list. One name that had been included from the beginning was Itzhak Stern, Oskar's most trusted advisor and friend during all his years in Krakow.

When the list was out of Oskar's hands more names were added by Marcel Goldberg, the personnel clerk at Plaszów. The

Plaszów authorities were busy with the job of closing the camp and would sign any list Goldberg gave them as long as there were not many more than 1,100 names on it. After adding his own name Goldberg, known as Lord of the Lists, took bribes to add more. 'For this list, it takes diamonds,' he told people.

After the war every survivor had a story about how this person or that one got on the list. Leopold Pfefferberg, for example, did not have any diamonds to give Goldberg, but with his trading skills he was able to get hold of a bottle of whisky. With this in hand he went to talk to Hans Schreiber, an SS officer who had an evil reputation but for some reason found Pfefferberg amusing and interesting. The Jew gave Schreiber the bottle and begged him to force Goldberg to add his and Mila's names to the list.

'Yes,' Schreiber agreed, 'the two of you must get on it.' And when the time came, the Pfefferbergs found themselves there. The mystery is why men like Schreiber did not ask themselves: *If this man and his wife are worth saving, why aren't the rest?*

The men on Schindler's list, including Marcel Goldberg, who must have left his bags of diamonds with someone in Krakow, climbed into the boxcars of a cattle train at the Plaszów station on Sunday, 15 October 1944. The women would leave a week later. The 800 Schindler men were kept separate on the train from an additional 1,300 prisoners who were heading for Gröss-Rosen. The Schindler Jews expected to be taken directly to Brinnlitz, and so they were fairly tolerant of the difficult conditions during their three-day journey.

The train moved slowly and snow was already falling in this part of Poland. Each prisoner had been given less than half a kilogram of bread to last the entire trip, and each boxcar had been provided with a single water bucket. Instead of a toilet the travellers had to use a corner of the floor, or the space in which they stood if their car was really crowded. But the Schindler men continued to feel hopeful about their destination: Brinnlitz and Herr Schindler.

Finally the train reached its destination late on the third day. The doors were unlocked and the SS guards ran among the prisoners shouting, 'Hurry up!' 'Everyone off the train!' 'Take off all your clothes. Everything must be disinfected.' The prisoners piled their clothes and shoes on the ground and looked around, realizing they were in the main square of the Gröss-Rosen Concentration Camp. Was a Schindler camp in Czechoslovakia just a dream?

There was no room in the prisoner barracks at Gröss-Rosen, and so the men were kept on the square all night with nothing to protect their bodies from the bitter weather. In later years when talking about those seventeen hours in the severe cold, survivors did not mention any deaths. Maybe life under the SS had made them tough enough to live through such horrors.

Towards eleven o'clock the next morning, the prisoners had all their hair shaved off by Ukrainian soldiers before they were taken to the showers.

Leopold Pfefferberg crowded into the shower with the others and looked up, wondering if it would be gas or water that came out. To everyone's relief it was water, and after washing the men were given striped prison uniforms and crowded into barracks. The SS guards made them sit in lines, one man backed up between the legs of the man behind him, his opened legs giving support to the man in front. By this method, 2,000 men were crowded into three barracks and covered every inch of the floor.

Each day the prisoners had to stand in silence for ten hours in the camp's main square. Then they were given thin soup in the evenings and had a little time to walk and talk together before going back at nine o'clock to their barracks and their odd sitting position for the night.

On the second day, an SS officer came to the barracks looking for the clerk who had been in charge of Schindler's list. Somehow it had not been sent with the prisoners from Plaszów.

Marcel Goldberg was led off to an office and asked to type out the list from memory. By the end of the day he had not finished the work and, back in the prisoners' barracks, he was surrounded by people making sure that he had remembered their names and begging him to include other friends and family members.

Then, on the third day, the 800 men of the re-written list were separated out from the mass on the square, taken to the showers for another wash, permitted to sit for a few hours and talk like villagers in front of their barracks, and at last marched to the railway track again.

Their train travelled 160 kilometres and the doors opened early in the morning of the second day at Zwittau station. The Schindler men and a few boys got off the train and were marched through the sleeping town. Zwittau had not been touched by the war; it looked as though it had been asleep since the late 1930s.

The group tramped five or six kilometres into the hills to the industrial village of Brinnlitz, where they saw the solid-looking buildings of the Hoffman factory, and to one side the Brinnlitz Labour Camp with watchtowers, a wire fence around it, and some barracks for the guards.

As they marched through the gate, Oskar Schindler appeared from the big building inside the fence, smiling and wearing a Sudeten country gentleman's hat. They were home again.

Chapter 11 To Hell and Back

Everything at the new Brinnlitz camp was paid for by Oskar Schindler. According to the Nazis this made sense since the factory owners would make impressive profits by taking advantage of cheap labour from the camps. In fact, Oskar did get some cement, petrol and fuel oil and fencing wire at very low prices before leaving Krakow, but he still had to pay wartime prices out of his own pocket for the materials he needed for everything else, from toilet huts and kitchens to watchtowers and his own apartment. He also had to be prepared for official visits from SS men like Commandant Hassebroeck, who left Brinnlitz with inspection fees in his pocket and his car packed with a supply of whisky, tea and enamelware.

Schindler spent his money enthusiastically, but his operation at Brinnlitz was unique because he knew he was not investing this money in a serious business. Four years earlier he had gone to Krakow to get rich, but in October of 1944 he had no plans for production or sales. His only goal was to save the lives of the 1,100 Jews on his list, but, of course, this was never an uncomplicated task.

One of Oskar's new complications at Brinnlitz was having his wife Emilie as part of his daily life again. The factory and sub-camp were too close to Zwittau for a good Catholic wife to live separately from her husband, so Emilie moved into Oskar's apartment inside the factory and found her own role at the camp, helping many people, especially the sick and lonely. The couple treated each other with respect, but it is doubtful that Oskar now became a better husband. He remained close friends with Ingrid, who had moved to Brinnlitz, and he continued to visit Victoria Klonowska, who was always ready to help her former boss in times of trouble, whenever he went to Krakow.

◆

At the Brinnlitz camp, Oskar told the men confidently that the women would be joining them almost immediately, but the Schindler women's journey was not as simple as Oskar had hoped. The 300 women and girls had left Plaszów in boxcars with 2,000 other female prisoners, but when the train doors opened they had found themselves in Auschwitz-Birkenau instead of Brinnlitz.

The Schindler group marched through the thick mud of Birkenau to the shower house, where they too were thankful that icy water rather than gas came out of the showers. Some of the other prisoners were taken away to get numbers tattooed on their arms. This was a good sign because it meant that the Nazis intended to use you, not feed you directly into the gas chambers. With a tattoo you could leave Birkenau and go to one of the Auschwitz labour camps, where there was at least a small chance of survival, but the Schindler women were not given tattoos. Instead they were ordered to dress and go to a barracks, where they found no beds, a wet dirt floor, no glass in the windows – it was a death house at the heart of Birkenau. On some days there were more than a quarter of a million prisoners in this one camp; there were thousands more in Auschwitz I and tens of thousands working in the industrial area named Auschwitz III.

The women from DEF had no idea about these numbers, but outside, looking towards the western horizon, they could see constant smoke rising from the four huge crematoria. They would not have guessed that, when the system worked well, 9,000 people could be gassed in one day.

The women were also not aware that the progress of the war had taken a new direction. The outside world learnt about the existence of the death camps when the Russians uncovered gas chambers, crematoria, human bones and Zyklon B at the Lublin camp. Himmler, who wanted to take Hitler's place after the war, announced that the gassing of Jews would stop, but he delayed giving the order to the Gestapo and the SS. Jews continued to be gassed until the middle of November 1944, and after that date they were either shot or allowed to die of disease.

The Schindler women knew nothing about these changes and lived every day with the threat of death by gassing; no industrial prisoners, even the ones on Schindler's list, were safe at Auschwitz. In fact, the previous year General Pohl had sent several trains full of Jewish workers from Berlin to I G Farben, but the trains had stopped at Auschwitz–Birkenau. Of the 1,750 male prisoners in the first train, 1,000 were immediately gassed. Of 4,000 in the next four trains, 2,500 went directly to the gas chambers. If the Auschwitz administration had not been careful with workers for Farben and General Pohl, how careful would they be about Jews who called themselves Schindler's group?

The doctors of Auschwitz walked through the camps daily looking for the old, the weak and the sick and sent them directly to the gas chambers. When the women saw the doctors coming, they would rub a bit of red mud on their cheeks and try to stand up straighter. If a woman fainted during an inspection, which could occur at any hour, the guards picked her up, dragged her to the electric fence and threw her on to it.

◆

In their first days at Brinnlitz the Schindler men were worried about their mothers, wives and daughters in Auschwitz. When Schindler appeared on the factory floor, they would gather round him and ask about the women. Oskar did not try to explain anything, but would simply say, 'I'm getting them out.'

In the middle of this worry and activity, Oskar was arrested for the third time. The Gestapo arrived at the factory unexpectedly one lunchtime.

In his office Oskar was questioned about his connections with Amon Goeth. 'I do have a few of Commandant's Goeth's suitcases here,' Oskar told the men. 'He asked me to keep them for him while he was in prison.'

And even though the Gestapo found nothing except Amon Goeth's non-military clothes in the suitcases, they arrested Oskar.

'You have no right to arrest him,' shouted Emilie Schindler. 'Explain what he has done. What is his crime? The people in Berlin won't be happy about this.'

'Darling, please, don't worry,' Oskar quietly advised his wife. 'But please call my friend Victoria Klonowska and cancel my appointments.' Emilie knew what this meant. Klonowska would do her trick with the telephone again, calling Oskar's important friends and relying on them to get him out of this mess.

The Gestapo men took Oskar back to Krakow by train, to the prison he had stayed in during his first arrest. Again he had a comfortable room, but this time he was genuinely frightened about what might happen. He knew that the Gestapo's methods for making prisoners confess were cruel and dangerous.

The next morning Oskar was questioned by twelve SS investigators. 'Commandant Goeth has said that you gave him money so that he would make life easier for the Jews. Is that true?' asked one of the investigators.

'I may have given him money,' said Oskar, 'but only as a loan.'

'Why would you give him a loan?' the investigator asked.

'My factory is part of an essential war industry,' said Oskar, using his usual defence. 'If I found out about a skilled metalworker at Plaszów, for example, and wanted him to work at DEF, I would want him sent to me as quickly as possible. Because of the Herr Commandant's help in these matters, I may have given him a loan.'

The investigators understood what Oskar was talking about: Amon Goeth had had to be paid for favours. What helped Oskar most when he faced the investigators was the fact that he had not done any business deals with Goeth. He had never had a share in his black market trading or in the small operations Goeth had set up inside Plaszów to make furniture, clothes and shoes. There were no letters or contracts to imply that the two men had been business partners, or even friends.

Oskar was so charming that the investigators wanted to believe his version of events. Also, Oskar's friends in high places supported him again. Colonel Erich Lange emphasized how important Herr Schindler's work was to the war effort, and Sussmuth reported that DEF was involved in the production of 'secret weapons', something that Hitler had talked about and promised, but which no one had actually seen.

Nevertheless, Oskar was not confident about the way the investigation was going. On about the fourth day one of the SS men visited him in his cell, not to question him but to spit at him and curse him for being a Jew-lover. Maybe it was a test planned by the SS, but it made Oskar nervous because he did not know how they expected him to react to these insults.

On the other hand, Oskar was also visited by the Krakow police chief, whose departing words were, 'Don't worry. We intend to get you out.' On the morning of the eighth day Oskar found himself outside the prison. When he arrived back at Brinnlitz, he was surprised and pleased to learn that Emilie had kept things going while he had been in prison, but he was also shocked to find that the women were still in the distant concentration camp.

◆

In October 1944 Auschwitz-Birkenau was ruled by Commandant Rudolf Höss, the camp's builder and the brain behind Zyklon B. According to the stories told by Schindler men and women long after the war, it was Höss himself that Oskar had to argue with for his 300 women, and, indeed, there is evidence proving that there was contact between the two men during this time, although the content of their communications is unknown. On the other hand, the story of Oskar sending a girl to Auschwitz-Birkenau is certain.

Itzhak Stern, the most reliable of witnesses, told this story years later in a public speech in Tel Aviv. After Oskar was released from prison, he and a group of the Schindler men were discussing what could be done about the women trapped in Auschwitz when one of Schindler's secretaries came into the office.

Oskar pointed to a huge diamond ring that he was wearing and said to the girl, 'Would you like to have this ring?'

The girl's eyes lit up and she said, 'I'd love to have it – it's the most beautiful ring I've ever seen, and the biggest diamond.'

'Take the list of women, pack a suitcase with the best food and drink you can find in my kitchen and go to Auschwitz. The commandant there has an eye for pretty women. If you bring the women back, you'll get this diamond.'

According to Stern the secretary went, and when she did not return after two days, Schindler himself went to Auschwitz to settle the matter. Others remember the story differently. Maybe the girl slept with the commandant and left a handful of diamonds on his pillow. Maybe the girl was a good friend of Emilie's. No one is positive about the details, but it is certain that Oskar sent a girl to Auschwitz and that she acted with courage.

When he arrived at the concentration camp, Oskar used his old argument about needing his highly trained workers for his essential industry.

'Just a moment,' said one of Höss's officials. 'I see the names of girls as young as nine years old on this list. Are you telling me that they are skilled metalworkers?'

'Of course,' replied Schindler confidently. 'They can polish the insides of weapons with their long, thin fingers. It is work that is beyond most adults.'

Schindler continued to argue his case, mainly by telephone. He knew that the women were getting weaker each day and soon no one would believe that they were strong enough to work in any factory. Even young women like Helen Hirsch and Mila Pfefferberg were suffering with terrible hunger, stomach problems and coughs.

Clara Sternberg, a Schindler woman in her early forties, had been put in the barracks for sick women at Auschwitz, and one morning after inspection she decided that she could not face another day. She had stopped believing that she would ever see her husband and teenage son at Brinnlitz, so she walked through the women's camp, looking for one of the many electric fences.

When she saw a woman from Plaszów, a Krakow woman like herself, Clara stopped her and asked, 'Where is an electric fence? Yesterday they were everywhere and today I can't find even one.'

It was a crazy question, but this was a crazy situation and Clara expected the woman to point the way to the wires. Fortunately for Clara, the woman gave her an odd, but sane reply.

'Don't kill yourself on the fence, Clara. If you do that, you'll never know what happened to you.'

Clara was not sure that she understood what the woman was talking about, but she turned around, went back to her barracks and did not try to kill herself again.

◆

While Oskar was away from Brinnlitz, trading enamelware, diamonds and cigarettes for drugs and medical equipment for his workers, an inspector arrived from Gröss-Rosen and walked through the factory with Josef Liepold, the new commandant. The inspector had orders from Berlin that all sub-camps had to be cleared of any children. The doctors at Auschwitz wanted them sent there to be used in their medical experiments.

The young boys at Oskar's factory were used to living a relatively normal life and were allowed to run and play throughout the factory, so the inspectors had no trouble finding most of them. The orders also required the children's parents to accompany them, so the fathers joined their captured sons for the trip to Auschwitz-Birkenau.

On the train from Zwittau to the concentration camp, the small group was guarded by a polite young SS sergeant. At one stop he even went to the station café and returned with biscuits and coffee for the prisoners. He started talking to two of the fathers, Henry Rosner and Dolek Horowitz, whose wives were at Auschwitz.

'I'm taking you to Auschwitz,' the kind sergeant said, 'and then I have to collect some women and bring them back to Brinnlitz.'

'This good gentleman is going to bring your mother back to Brinnlitz,' they told their sons, and the thrilling news spread through the Schindler group.

The two men also dared to ask the sergeant for a favour: would he give letters to their wives from them? The sergeant gave them some of his own writing paper and promised to deliver the letters to Manci Rosner and Regina Horowitz.

Later in the journey Henry's son, Olek, began to cry as he leaned against his father's arm.

'Son, what's the matter?' asked Henry.

'I don't want you to die because of me,' he said. 'You should be back in Brinnlitz.'

The SS sergeant leaned over with tears in his eyes too. 'I know what will happen,' he said gently to Henry. 'We've lost the war. You'll get the tattoo and you'll live to the end.'

Henry Rosner was grateful to the sergeant, but he got the impression that the man was making promises to himself as well as to Olek. Perhaps in five years' time the sergeant would remember his words and be comforted.

◆

On the afternoon of the day on which Clara Sternberg had gone looking for an electric wire, she heard talking and laughter coming from the direction of the Schindler barracks. She crawled out of the damp building where she had been put and saw the Schindler women standing outside the camp's inner fence. They looked as thin and old as everyone else in the camp, but they were chatting and laughing like schoolgirls. Women from the other barracks stared at these cheerful women, acting so strangely for camp prisoners.

Clara Sternberg knew that her name was on the list, and she decided to act. A fence, not an electric fence, but a strong one with eighteen parallel wires with gaps of only about twenty centimetres, stood between Mrs Sternberg and her friends. According to witnesses, Mrs Sternberg tore her way through the fence, ripping her thin dress and her flesh, and rejoined the Schindler women. The guards were too surprised to stop her.

The group of women were taken to the washhouse and were showered and shaved before being marched with no clothes on to another barracks, where they were given clothes from the recently dead. Still they remained in a good mood, chatting and modelling the clothes for each other.

But the women grew quiet as they walked towards the train; it was always a frightening experience to be packed into the blackness of a boxcar. That morning Niusia Horowitz, the only daughter of Dolek Horowitz, found a corner in the boxcar where a board had come loose, and from there she could see what was going on behind the fence of the men's camp. She saw something unusual: there was a small group of boys waving at the train. Niusia thought that one of the boys looked a lot like her six-year-old brother Richard, who was safe in Brinnlitz. And the boy at his side looked like their cousin Olek Rosner. Then, of course, she understood: it *was* Richard, and it *was* Olek.

Niusia called to her mother, and the women pushed her to the corner of the crowded boxcar so that they could look out. Soon Regina Horowitz and Manci Rosner, the boys' mothers, were crying loudly, not understanding what this meant for their sons. The door of the boxcar opened and a young guard shouted, 'Who is making all this noise?'

Regina and Manci pushed through the crowd of women again and Manci tried to explain, 'My child is over there behind the fence. I want to show him that I'm still alive.'

'Get off the train, just you two,' the guard ordered. 'What are your names?'

When the women answered, the guard pulled something out of his pocket – not a gun, as the women had expected, but a letter for each of them. Then he told them about his trip to Auschwitz with their husbands and sons.

'Could you let us get down under the train for a minute or two?' asked Manci. Sometimes this was allowed if the train was delayed and the prisoners needed to use the toilet.

With the guard's permission, the two women quickly got under the train and Manci let out the whistle she had used at Plaszów to communicate with her family. Soon the two boys saw them and were waving to their mothers. Olek held his arm up and pulled back his sleeve to show his mother that he had a tattoo; Richard showed his too. They were 'permanent'.

Then Olek held out his hand and showed his mother a few little potatoes he had: 'Don't worry about me being hungry.'

Richard, the younger of the two boys, showed that he had some potatoes too, but he could not stop himself from saying, 'Mama, I'm so hungry.'

Henry Rosner and Dolek Horowitz arrived at the fence while the women were still outside the train. By now the wives had read the letters from their husbands and understood the situation.

'The tattoo!' Henry called proudly. His wife was happy about that, but worried because she could see that he was cold and sweating at the same time, being worked to death.

There was little time now before the train left, and the guard wanted the women to get back on the train. 'Look after Niusia,' Dolek called out, trying to sound cheerful, and then the families were separated again. Nothing could surprise them any more.

As the train moved away from Auschwitz, the women knew that this was their last chance. Many of them would die within days if they did not get some food and rest; another concentration camp would finish them all.

In the cold dawn of the second day, the train stopped and the women were ordered out. They climbed out of the boxcar and smelled the air, which was painfully cold but fresh and clean. They were marched to a large gate and behind it they could see several large chimneys and a group of SS guards.

'They've brought us all this way to send us up a chimney anyway,' a girl beside Mila Pfefferberg cried.

'No,' said Mila, 'they wouldn't waste their time like that.'

As they got closer to the gate, they saw Herr Schindler standing among the Brinnlitz SS men. He stepped forward and the lines of women stopped. They could neither believe their eyes, nor could they speak; it was like seeing a ghost.

Then Oskar spoke to the women, even though Commandant Liepold was there with him. 'When you go inside the building you'll find soup and bread waiting for you. You have nothing more to worry about. You're with me now.'

Years later one of the women tried to explain their feelings that morning: 'He was our father, he was our mother, he was our only faith. We could always depend on him.'

The Schindler men stood on the balcony of the building as the women passed below, each man searching for the face of his mother, wife, daughter or friend. Because the women had no hair and many of them were very ill, they were not all easily recognizable, but it was an amazing sight. There had never been and never would be another Auschwitz rescue like this one.

Many of the women had to go directly to the factory's medical unit to be treated for all kinds of problems. Emilie Schindler worked quietly in this part of Oskar's kingdom, feeding and comforting the sick and dying.

Chapter 12 Life in the Kingdom of Oskar Schindler

Oskar Schindler ran his little kingdom at Brinnlitz under the careful watch of Commandant Josef Liepold in his office outside the gate of the DEF building, and under the official control of Commandant Hassebroeck at Gröss-Rosen. Somehow, though, even with watchful Nazi eyes observing every move, Schindler managed to do things *his* way.

If it was discovered that a prisoner had brought typhoid fever into the Brinnlitz camp, not only would that prisoner be shot, but also the camp would be closed and the rest of the prisoners would be sent to the typhoid barracks of Birkenau to die.

On one of Oskar's morning visits to the medical unit in the camp, one of the Jewish doctors told him that there were two possible cases of typhoid fever among the women. The disease was carried from person to person by louse bites, and it was impossible to control the huge population of lice that lived on the prisoners.

So Oskar ordered the doctors to isolate the two women by putting them in the basement. He then ordered his workers to begin building a de-lousing unit with showers, a laundry and a disinfection room as quickly as possible; in this way he stopped the spread of the disease before it had a chance to get started. Regular meals also took care of most of the prisoners' stomach complaints. In all of war-torn Europe, only the Jews who were lucky enough to be in Brinnlitz were fed enough to live on.

'You have to remember,' said a prisoner of Oskar's camp years later, 'that Brinnlitz was hard. But compared to any other camp, it was heaven!'

'And Schindler? Did he eat the same meals as the prisoners?'

The former prisoner laughed at such a question. 'Schindler? Why would Schindler cut his rations? He was the Herr Director.'

After a pause, the man continued, 'You don't understand. We were grateful to be there. There was nowhere else to be.'

After finishing work on the new de-lousing unit one evening, Leopold Pfefferberg and another male prisoner climbed to the top of the DEF building to bathe in a water tank on the roof. The water was warm up there from the heat of the machines, and when you climbed into the tank you could not be seen from the floor.

Dragging themselves up, the two prisoners were amazed to find the tank already occupied. Huge Oskar Schindler was sharing the bath with a beautiful blonde SS girl, whose healthy golden breasts floated on the surface. The two men apologized and left, shaking their heads and laughing like schoolboys.

Soon afterwards Schindler wandered into one of his workshops to talk to Moshe Bejski, a young artist.

'Could you make a rubber stamp like the one used on these official papers?' Oskar asked, as he showed Bejski a document from the Food and Agriculture Department in Krakow.

Bejski began his new job immediately and became an expert at copying Nazi stamps which Oskar could then use on all sorts of official documents. Prisoners could now do work outside the factory, such as driving by truck to Brno or Olomouc to collect loads of bread, black market petrol, flour or cigarettes.

In the Krakow years DEF had produced a vast quantity of enamelware and a smaller amount of weapons which had made a fortune for Oskar Schindler, but the factory in Brinnlitz produced nothing of any worth at all. As Oskar would claim, 'We had difficulties with the production of weapons and bullets.'

Because DEF did not produce anything that was exactly right, Oskar was getting a bad name at the Weapons Ministry, and other factory managers and owners were getting more and more angry with DEF. The factory system was planned so that one workshop made bullets and another made guns, so if Oskar's prisoners made bullets that were the wrong size, for example, both DEF and the factory that made the weapons for those bullets looked bad.

Oskar celebrated when his bullets or guns did not work because he did not want to help the Nazis kill more people, but as this went on, he also had to find more and more clever ways to protect his business and his Jews. Even in 1945 there was a series of inspections at DEF when Nazi officials and engineers marched through the factory with their checklists. Oskar used his old tricks and started these official visits with a very good lunch and several bottles of excellent wine. In the Third Reich there were no longer as many good meals for minor officials as there had been. Prisoners standing at their machines would report that the uniformed inspectors smelled of alcohol and were unsteady on their feet as they tried to concentrate on their task.

The prisoners also had their own tricks. The skilled electricians and engineers among them adjusted the machines so that they looked normal and efficient, but they did not perform properly. Some machines, for example, did not reach the correct temperature, or the size of a bullet was just a tiny bit too big. These problems could not be seen in an inspection, but they meant that DEF never produced any workable weapons or bullets.

There were complaints about the Brinnlitz factory from local officials as well, and Oskar regularly gave important men from the surrounding areas a tour of the factory and a good dinner. But after his third arrest Commandant Liepold and the Hoffman brothers, owners of the DEF building, wrote to every Nazi office they could think of to complain about Oskar Schindler and his morals, his law-breaking and his love of Jews. Oskar heard about the attacks on him and invited two of his old friends to Brinnlitz.

The first was Ernst Hahn, second in command of the Berlin office of services to SS families, and with him he brought Franz Bosch, a frequent guest at Amon Goeth's parties at Plaszów. Both men were famous drunks and both of them loved the sociable

Oskar Schindler and saw him as a man, like them, who knew how to enjoy the finer things in life.

The two men arrived looking like leaders from the early grand days of the Nazi Party in their splendid Nazi uniforms, complete with military decorations and ribbons. Commandant Liepold was invited to join them for dinner and felt like a schoolboy at the grown-ups' table. He left knowing that if he wrote complaining letters to distant authorities, they were likely to land on the desk of an old drinking companion of the Herr Director, and that could prove to be more dangerous for him than for Schindler.

The next morning Oskar was seen driving through Zwittau, laughing and joking with these elegant, handsome men from Berlin. He hated both Hahn and Bosch, but he was an expert at acting whatever role was necessary to protect his workers. The local Nazis stood on the pavements and waved as this wonderful display of Reich power passed by.

◆

Down in the basement of DEF, one of the two women who had had typhoid fever still remained isolated. Luisa's fevers kept returning. She remained in the basement, well fed and well looked after, but as white as a ghost and still carrying the infection. She understood that she was in the only space in Europe in which she would be allowed to live.

One morning as Luisa lay in her bed, she heard the heavy boots of three men coming down the stairs and she tensed, expecting the worst. It was the Herr Director with two official inspectors from Gröss-Rosen. Luisa was partly hidden behind a large heater, but Schindler did not try to hide her. Instead he came and stood at the end of her bed and talked about her as if she was not there.

'This is a Jewish girl,' Schindler said in a bored voice. 'I didn't want to put her in the medical unit. She's not infectious, but she has something serious. The doctors say she won't last more than thirty-six hours.'

Then Oskar ignored the girl and told the men about the machines and equipment around them. Luisa closed her eyes and lay very still, but as the men began to climb the stairs she cautiously opened her eyes. Herr Schindler looked back and gave her a quick smile. It was the kind of victory that excited him and kept him working every day for his Jews.

In the spring of 1945, after six months in the basement, Luisa walked out of DEF and into an altered world to continue her life.

◆

Oskar's old drinking friends sometimes thought of him as the victim of a Jewish fever, and they were not using literary language. They believed that he had a real disease, one that he had caught and could not be blamed for. They even believed that this brain fever was highly infectious, and they pointed to men like Sussmuth as proof of this.

Over the winter of 1944–45, Oskar and Sussmuth managed to get 3,000 more women out of some of the biggest camps and into sub-camps in Czechoslovakia by finding small factories which needed workers. With Oskar's influence and charm, and Sussmuth's clever paperwork, the pair convinced the authorities to send groups of 300–500 women at a time into typically tiny rural factories, where they had a chance of escaping the death orders that reached the bigger camps in the spring of 1945.

While this was going on, Oskar continued to search for other ways to rescue more Jews; through Sussmuth again, he applied for an extra thirty metalworkers. Eventually he got these thirty men, but not before another dramatic journey.

Moshe Henigman, one of the prisoners, wrote about this trip after the war: 'A short time after Christmas 1944, 10,000 prisoners from Auschwitz III were lined up and marched away towards Gröss-Rosen. We heard that we were being taken to work in the area's factory camps, but if the Nazis wanted us to work, they didn't plan the journey very well. It was a bitterly cold time of year and we had no food as we walked along. At the beginning of each stage of the march, anyone who had trouble walking or had a cough was shot. After ten days there were only 1,200 of the original 10,000 left alive, and each day as we continued, the weak were separated out and killed.

'Then one day thirty of us heard our names called, and we were put into a boxcar. We were even given food for the trip, which was unbelievable. Then we arrived at Brinnlitz and thought we'd died and gone to heaven. Schindler even let us rest and build up our strength before going to work. After what we had been through, it was hard to believe that men like him still existed.'

Dr Steinberg, working at a small labour camp in the Sudeten hills, also had a story to tell about Schindler's kind but dangerous behaviour. 'I was the doctor at a camp which made aircraft parts. There were about 400 prisoners, with a very poor diet and an extremely heavy workload.

'I heard rumours that this man Schindler was running a civilized camp at Brinnlitz, so I managed to get a factory truck to use and went to visit him. I told him about the conditions in my camp and, without hesitating, he worked out a way for me to visit Brinnlitz twice a week and get extra food. I don't know exactly how many kilograms of food I picked up over those months, but if the Brinnlitz supplies had not been available, at least fifty more of our prisoners would have died by spring.'

By January 1945 the Nazis were closing down some of the factories inside Auschwitz itself, and in the middle of that month 120 workers from the cement factory were thrown into two boxcars. They travelled for ten days without food and with the doors of the train frozen shut. A boy remembered that they scratched the ice off the inside walls to get enough water to keep themselves alive. The train stopped at Birkenau and at other camps, but the doors of their boxcars remained shut; they had no industrial value and the commandants did not want the responsibility of either housing or killing them.

Finally, on a freezing morning at the end of January, the two boxcars were abandoned in the rail yards at Zwittau. It was probably Oskar's brother-in-law who telephoned him to report cries and scratching noises from inside the cars. Oskar told him to move the two boxcars to Brinnlitz.

Leopold Pfefferberg was called to bring his tools and cut the frozen doors open. In each boxcar, they saw a pile of stiff and twisted bodies which no longer looked human. The hundred survivors each weighed less than thirty-four kilograms, they smelled terrible and their skin had turned black from the cold. The condition of both the dead and the living reminded the Brinnlitz Jews of what was happening outside Schindler's kingdom. When they were inside the factory, Emilie Schindler and the doctors made sure that these 'workers' all survived.

◆

Into this strange factory which employed the weak and hungry and which produced nothing useful came Amon Goeth in the early days of 1945. He had been released from prison because of serious health problems, although the SS were continuing their investigation of his affairs. No one was sure what his motives were for this visit. Was he looking for a managerial job in Oskar's factory? Did he need money and want a loan? Had Oskar acted as his agent in a business deal? Or was he just hoping to find someone who was still his friend?

A different Amon Goeth walked through the factory that day. He was much thinner and his face showed the signs of illness and worry, but for the former residents of Plaszów this man still represented evil. Some people turned their heads away from him and spat; others, like Helen Hirsch, could not move when they saw him. Surely the former commandant had no power in Oskar's kingdom, but the prisoners could not be sure. He was still Amon Goeth and he had a presence, a habit of authority. Thirty years later Leopold Pfefferberg said, 'When you saw Goeth, even in your dreams, you saw death.'

Everyone felt a sense of relief when Oskar led him through the factory on the third day on his way back to the station at Zwittau. The prisoners were now rid of their old commandant, and at the time of Oskar's thirty-seventh birthday on 28 April 1945 he was scheming to get rid of Commandant Liepold as well.

In the week before the birthday celebrations an order from Hassebroeck, who, as we know, was the commandant of Gröss-Rosen and in charge of Brinnlitz and 103 other small camps, had reached Liepold's office. The order instructed Liepold to get rid of all his Jewish prisoners by shooting the old and weak immediately and marching the others out of the area in the direction of Mauthausen. The Nazis did not want the approaching Russian army to discover the camps or the prisoners.

It was fortunate for the prisoners in this new phase of danger that neither they nor Liepold ever knew anything about this order. Mietek Pemper, whom we have met as one of Amon Goeth's secretaries, was now working in Commandant Liepold's office and did not hesitate to read his boss's mail. After seeing Hassebroeck's order, Pemper took it directly to Herr Schindler.

'All right,' Oskar said after reading the communication, 'then we must say goodbye to Commandant Liepold.'

Schindler knew that Liepold was the only SS officer in Brinnlitz who was capable of carrying out this death sentence. His deputy, an older man named Motzek, would never be able to murder a large number of human beings so coldly.

Feeling certain of this, Oskar decided to get Liepold out of Brinnlitz and leave Motzek in charge. He wrote letters of complaint against the commandant to important friends in Berlin and to Hassebroeck. He accused the commandant of unnecessarily severe treatment of the prisoners and of threatening to kill them all immediately. Then he reminded the men he was writing to that his labourers were working on secret weapons, and that they were necessary for a final German victory. Even though Hassebroeck was responsible for thousands of deaths and believed that all Jews should be killed when the Russians came near, he was against any of his commandants making a special case of his own prisoners.

Schindler noted that Liepold kept saying that he would like to be in the real fighting, rather than sitting behind a desk. Two days after Oskar's birthday, Liepold received his orders to join an army unit at the battlefront. Schindler's Jews were now safer under their latest commandant, Herr Motzek, who knew nothing about any recent orders from Hassebroeck.

◆

On 28 April Oskar received a special hand-made box and birthday wishes from the workers and provided two truckloads of white bread for them. Oskar's serious mood was reflected in a speech he made that night to his prisoners and staff as well as to the SS. Leopold Pfefferberg later remembered that he looked around nervously at the SS men with their guns and thought: *They will kill this man, and then everything will fall apart.*

Schindler's birthday speech contained two main promises. First, that the war and the rule of terror was ending. He spoke as if the SS men standing against the walls were also prisoners who longed for liberation. Then he promised that he would stay at Brinnlitz until the war was officially over. 'And five minutes longer,' he added, promising the Jews that he would not allow them to be taken into the woods to be shot before the Nazis departed.

Oskar delivered his speech calmly, but he later admitted how worried he had been during those last days about what actions might be taken by the SS, or by German army units or advancing Russian soldiers; he knew that these groups were capable of anything. But with their stomachs full and their Herr Director speaking, the prisoners did not sense the terror Oskar felt.

Chapter 13 The Gates Are Opened

Both Oskar and a group of prisoners had radios and were able to keep in touch with what was happening during the final days of the war. They knew that Russian soldiers were shooting non-military German citizens, but they believed the war would end before any Russian army units could reach the Zwittau area. The Jewish prisoners had hoped that the Sudeten area would be captured by the Americans, but the news they heard indicated that the Russians would reach them first. Nevertheless, the group of prisoners closest to Oskar were working on a letter in Hebrew to explain Oskar's actions during the war. They hoped that he would be able to present this letter to American forces, with their significant number of Jewish soldiers, including army rabbis, and that this would guarantee his safety.

Oskar heard the news of the German surrender on the radio in the small hours of 7 May. The war in Europe would cease at midnight on the following night, Tuesday, 8 May 1945.

At midday the next day Schindler stopped work in the factory and everyone listened to Winston Churchill's victory speech as it was broadcast in English from London. A few of the workers understood what Churchill was saying and the news spread quickly. As the SS men learnt what had happened, they started to look away from the prisoners and the camp and began worrying about the approaching Russians and the dangers the world beyond the camp might hold for them. Nevertheless, they remained conscious of their duty and stayed at their posts until midnight.

In the long hours leading up to the peace one of the prisoners, a jeweller named Licht, had been working on a gift for Schindler. The prisoners knew that Oskar and Emilie would have to leave Brinnlitz as quickly as possible after midnight, but they wanted to mark this departure with a short ceremony and a special gift.

Licht was making a gold ring with these words on the inner circle: *He who saves a single life, saves the entire world* – the Talmudic verse Itzhak Stern had quoted to Oskar in the director's office at Buchheister's in October of 1939. But where had he found the gold? Old Mr Jereth, who had helped Oskar find the wood for his first sub-camp, insisted that Licht use his gold teeth. 'Without Oskar Schindler,' Mr Jereth said, 'my gold teeth would be in some heap in a Gestapo storehouse, with the teeth of thousands of other Jews.'

Everyone was looking for ways to help the Schindlers. Other prisoners took apart Oskar's luxury car and hid his diamonds inside the doors and under the seats.

Six hours before midnight Oskar called his prisoners and staff to another assembly, and the SS again stood along the walls with their guns. The Herr Director wanted to make a final speech about the new world they would all soon enter.

'The unconditional surrender of Germany,' he said, 'has just been announced. After six years of cruel murder, we cry for the victims, and Europe begins to return to peace and order. I ask all of you who have worried with me through many hard years to act now as civilized, decent men and women. The soldiers at the front, as well as the little man who has done his duty, are not responsible for what a group, calling itself German, has done.

'Millions of Jews have been murdered – your parents, children, brothers and sisters – and many Germans have fought against this killing, and even today there are millions of Germans who do not know about the horrors committed in their name.

'I beg you to leave justice to the authorities, to tell your stories in the courts. Do not commit acts of revenge or terror. For your own safety, keep order and act with understanding towards the people outside these gates.

'Do not thank me for your survival. Thank your own people who worked day and night. Thank Itzhak Stern and Mietek Pemper and others, who thought about you and worried about you every day, and faced death for you at every moment. With their guidance, continue to make only honourable decisions.'

The prisoners thought Oskar was walking on dangerous ground when he turned his attention to the SS men. 'I would like to thank the SS guards for acting in an extraordinarily good and correct manner in this camp.' If the SS accepted Oskar's praise, then there would be nothing left for them to do except to walk away.

'In conclusion,' Oskar ended, 'I request you all to keep a three-minute silence, in memory of the countless victims among you who have died in these cruel years.'

After the three minutes the SS left the hall quickly, and the prisoners asked Oskar for a few minutes of his time before he packed and left. Licht's ring was presented, and Oskar spent some time admiring it and showing the verse to Emilie while Itzhak Stern translated it for her. Then Oskar became very serious as he slowly placed the ring on his finger. Though nobody quite understood it, it was the moment in which the Jews became themselves again, and in which Oskar Schindler became dependent on their gifts.

The world was at peace, but none of the people inside Brinnlitz camp had a clear idea of what that meant for them. Over the past year Oskar had built up a store of weapons which he now passed out among the prisoners, who were glad to have some protection against the SS guards. But they need not have worried because the SS were ready to give up their own weapons and hurry towards their homes. When midnight came, there were no SS men or women in the camp, not even Commandant Motzek.

Now it was time for the Schindlers to depart, but first Oskar called Bankier and gave him the key to a private storeroom. It contained eighteen truckloads of high quality fabric, thread and shoes, which Oskar had agreed to store for the Nazi Weapons Department. Now this huge supply of goods – estimated to be worth 150,000 American dollars – would give the prisoners something with which to start their journey into freedom. Some of them made travelling clothes out of the fabric, others saved theirs to trade with as they moved out of the camp. Each prisoner was also given a ration of cigarettes and a bottle of whisky; these too were items which could be traded.

Oskar and Emilie wore the striped uniforms of prisoners as they said goodbye and climbed into their car with one of the prisoners as driver. Eight other Jewish men had volunteered to follow the Schindlers in a truck loaded with food, and with cigarettes and alcohol for trading. Oskar was anxious to leave because of the threat that the Russians could arrive at any time, but still he gave Stern and Bankier instructions until the last moment. The prisoners watched as the car and truck rolled through the gates. After so many promises, they now began to realize that they had to bear the weight and uncertainty of their own future.

The prisoners did not move out of the camp for three days as they tried to make certain that the world outside was safe for them. They remembered that the only time they had seen the SS show fear, apart from their anxiety in the last few days, had been when typhoid fever broke out. So on the morning after the Schindlers left they hung typhoid fever signs on the gate and along the fences.

Three Czech soldiers arrived at the gate that first afternoon and talked through the fence to the men on guard. 'It's all over now,' they said. 'You're free to walk out whenever you want.'

'We'll go when the Russians arrive,' said the guards. 'Until then we're staying inside.' Schindler's Jews wanted to be certain that the last German unit had gone. The Czechs walked away.

In fact, the Brinnlitz prisoners watched a German unit drive down the road from the direction of Zwittau later that day. Before they were out of sight, one of the German soldiers turned and fired his gun into the camp. A girl was slightly wounded by flying pieces of bullet, but her injury was not serious and no one else was hit.

They were also visited by five young German soldiers on SS motorbikes. When they turned off their engines and walked towards the gate, several of the men inside wanted to shoot them, but cooler heads persuaded them to wait and see what the soldiers wanted. 'We need petrol,' said the oldest of the Germans. 'Have you got any we can have?'

Leopold Pfefferberg argued that it was better to supply them with some fuel and send them on their way than to start a fight.

'I hope you realize there's typhoid fever here,' said Pfefferberg in German, pointing to the signs.

This seemed to impress the soldiers, who had no desire to add fever to their troubles. When the cans of petrol were brought to them, they thanked the prisoners politely and left as quickly and quietly as possible. This was the prisoners' last meeting with anyone from Henrich Himmler's special army.

On the third day a single Russian officer rode into the camp on horseback, and after a short conversation half in Russian, half in Polish, he asked for a chair. Standing on it, so that the prisoners could see and hear him, the officer gave them the standard liberation speech in Russian: 'You are free to go to town, to move in any direction you choose. You must not take revenge. We will find your enemies and punish them in a just and fair court.' He got down from the chair and smiled. He pointed to himself and said in old-fashioned Hebrew that he was Jewish too. Now the conversation became friendly.

'Have you been to Poland?' someone asked.

'Yes,' the officer admitted, 'I've just come from Poland.'

'Are there any Jews left up there?'

'I saw none, but I heard there are still a few Jews at Auschwitz,' the Russian reported. Before he left he promised to send them some bread and horsemeat. 'But you should see what they have in the town here,' he suggested.

As the Russian officer had urged them, the Brinnlitz prisoners began to move out of the camp. Their first experiences of the world outside were a mixture of the positive and the negative. A grocer offered some of the boys a bag of sugar he had been hiding in his storeroom. The boys could not resist the sweet taste and ate the sugar until they were sick, learning that they had to approach their freedom more gradually.

On Mila Pfefferberg's first visit to the village of Brinnlitz, a Czech soldier stopped two Sudeten girls and made them take off their shoes so that Mila, who had only an old pair of boots, could select the pair which fitted her best. Mila felt embarrassed by this sort of choice, and after the soldier had walked away she hurried after the girls and gave the shoes back. The Sudeten girls, Mila said, would not even speak to her.

Some of the families began to find their way to the West – to parts of Europe, to North and South America; others made plans to go to Palestine and settle with other Jews. Husbands and wives found their way to pre-arranged meeting places; others went to the Red Cross for news of family members.

Regina Horowitz and her daughter Niusia took three weeks to travel from Brinnlitz to Krakow to wait for their family. Dolek arrived but he had no news of little Richard, who had been taken away from him with a group of children several months previously. Then one day in the summer of that year Regina saw the film of Auschwitz which the Russians had made and were showing without charge in Polish cinemas.

'It's my son, it's my son!' Regina screamed when she saw Richard looking out from behind the fences. Through a Jewish rescue organization the parents learnt that Richard had been adopted by some old friends who thought Regina and Dolek were dead. He was returned to them, but he was now a nervous child and had terrible dreams because of what he had seen in the camps.

◆

After leaving, Oskar's group were stopped on the first day by Czech soldiers. One of the prisoners explained that they were all prisoners from the Brinnlitz labour camp: 'We escaped and took this truck and the director's car.'

'Do you have any weapons?' the Czech officer asked.

'Yes, we have a gun for protection,' the prisoner answered.

'Give it to us. You'll be safer without it if the Russians stop you. Your prison clothes are your best defence,' explained the officer. Then he directed them to the Czech Red Cross in the next town. 'They will give you a safe place to sleep for tonight.'

When the Brinnlitz car and truck reached the town, the Red Cross officials suggested that the safest place for the Schindlers and the nine young men to sleep would be in the town jail. So they took their few pieces of luggage into the jail for the night, leaving the car and truck in the town square.

When they returned to their vehicles in the morning, they found that everything had been taken – not only the hidden diamonds and food and drink, but also the tyres and the engines.

They could only continue their journey by train and on foot. They wanted to go towards Linz, where they hoped to find some American military units, and as they walked through a wooded area they met a group of American soldiers.

'Don't move,' said the leader of the group, after he heard Oskar's story. He drove away without explanation but returned within half an hour with a group of Jewish American soldiers and even a rabbi. They were very friendly and kind to the nine prisoners, who were the first Jewish concentration camp survivors they had seen. When Oskar showed the rabbi the letter from his workers, there were many tears as well as handshaking and clapping. Schindler and his party spent two days on the Austrian frontier as special guests of the American rabbi and the military commander. Then they were given an old ambulance to drive to Linz in Upper Austria.

From Linz, where the group reported to the American authorities, they travelled to Ravensburg. Again the Americans listened to their stories of Plaszów, Gröss-Rosen, Auschwitz and Brinnlitz before finding a bus for them to drive to Constanz, on the Swiss border. They believed the Schindlers would be safer in Switzerland, and then they and the prisoners could begin to make their own plans for the rest of their lives.

They reached the border and crossed into Switzerland, but they were then stopped and put in jail. They were not sure which story to tell: the truth or that the Schindlers were also Jewish prisoners. After several days the whole truth came out and local officials welcomed them and moved them to a fine hotel for several days of rest, paid for by the French military government.

By the time Oskar sat down to dinner with his wife and friends on that first night at the hotel, he had no money or diamonds left, but he was eating well with members of his 'family'. He did not know it then, but this would be the pattern for the rest of his life.

Chapter 14 The Final Years

Oskar Schindler lived for almost three more decades after the war, but, as Emilie Schindler said in 1973, 'Oskar had done nothing impressive with his life before the war and has done nothing special since.' He was fortunate, therefore, that in that short fierce period between 1939 and 1945 he had met people who had stirred him to use his deeper talents.

Between the end of the war and 1949 Oskar and Emilie lived in Germany, often staying with Schindler Jews who had returned to Munich. They lived very modestly; they had traded the last of their jewellery for food and drink and the Russians had taken Oskar's property in both Poland and Sudetenland. Still he was always as generous as possible with the Brinnlitz survivors who had become his family.

Many of the survivors from Plaszów and Brinnlitz were invited to attend the final trial of Amon Goeth, one of the first trials for war crimes brought by the Polish government. They found the former commandant thin from illness but still unwilling to accept any guilt for the killings at Plaszów. 'All orders for each death and transportation were signed by my superiors,' Goeth claimed, 'and were therefore *their* crimes, not mine.'

The judges listened to Goeth but they also listened to different accounts from survivors, including Mietek Pemper and Helen Hirsch, who gave clear details of Amon Goeth's crimes. Goeth was hanged in Krakow on 13 September 1946.

Towards the end of the forties Oskar was looking for a new business, something that would give him the kind of opportunities for success that he had found in Krakow in 1939. He decided to farm in Argentina, but he had no money to support this plan. However, an international Jewish organization stepped in to help him, based on his wartime activities as owner and director of 'the only two labour factories and sub-camps in the Nazi-occupied territories where a Jew was never killed, or even beaten, but was always treated as a human being.'

With 15,000 American dollars from this organization, the Schindlers sailed for Argentina in 1949, taking half a dozen families of Schindler Jews with them and paying the fares for many of them. They settled on a farm in Buenos Aires province and stayed there for a decade, but for many reasons the farm failed and the Schindlers went bankrupt. Perhaps Oskar's skills needed to be balanced with the more serious business sense of men like Itzhak Stern and Abraham Bankier.

By the beginning of the sixties Oskar was back in Germany and Emilie was still living in Argentina; they would never live together again. With 'loans' from a number of Schindler Jews Oskar tried to set up a cement factory, but soon he had gone bankrupt again.

In 1961, hearing that he was in trouble, the Schindler Jews in Israel invited Oskar to visit them at their expense. He was welcomed enthusiastically, and even though he looked older and heavier, the survivors were glad to see that he was still the same charming, sociable Herr Director at the series of parties and receptions held in his honour.

On Oskar's fifty-third birthday he was formally honoured with love and thanks in Tel Aviv in the Park of Heroes, where he was described as the man who had saved the lives of more than 1,200 prisoners at the Brinnlitz Concentration Camp. Ten days later in Jerusalem he was declared an Honourable Person and invited to plant a tree beside those of other honourable Germans, including Julius Madritsch and Raimund Titsch, owner and manager of the Madritsch Factory, where Jews had also been fed and protected.

The publicity Oskar received in Israel often made his life more difficult in Germany, where some people continued to hate him for being a Jew-lover. These attacks increased his need to depend on the Jewish survivors for his emotional and financial security. For the rest of his life he spent about half of every year in Israel, being treated like an honoured member of the family, and the other half in a small, dark apartment near the railway station in Frankfurt.

The Schindler Jews never forgot him, and worried that he often seemed discouraged and lonely and always short of money. Leopold Pfefferberg urged other survivors now living in the United States to contribute one day's pay a year to Schindler. Others, including Itzhak Stern and Moshe Bejski, persuaded the West German government to provide him with a decent pension based on his wartime heroism, the property he had lost and his poor health. In addition to the pension, the German government also officially recognized Schindler's noble acts during the war years.

As he entered his sixties, Oskar was still living and drinking like a young man although he was very ill with heart problems. He was working for several Jewish charities, and wherever he travelled he was well taken care of by his children, the survivors. But now they had become more like his parents, and they were concerned about his health and happiness.

Back in Germany one day in the autumn of 1974 Oskar fainted in his small apartment in Frankfurt, and he died in hospital on 9 October. A month later, according to his wishes, his body was carried through the crowded streets of the old city of Jerusalem and buried there. A crowd of Schindler Jews can be seen in the newspaper photographs of the ceremony.

He was grieved for on every continent.

ACTIVITIES

Before you read

1 What have you learnt about the treatment of Jews by Hitler and the Nazi government of Germany during the Second World War through books, films or TV programmes?

2 Find the words in *italics* in your dictionary. They are all used in the story. Decide if each sentence is true or false.

   a *Black market* trading is legal.

   b People in *concentration camps* are not there by choice.

   c Most people would keep *enamelware* and *rations* in the kitchen.

   d The most desirable property in any city is in a *ghetto*.

   e It is an act of war when one country *invades* another.

   f Sane, dull people are ruled by their *passions*.

   g *Sociable* people make a habit of refusing invitations.

3 Find the words in *italics* in your dictionary and answer the questions.

   a What is the difference between a person who is morally *bankrupt* and a person who is financially bankrupt?

   b Name three animals that are in danger of *extinction*.

   c In which religion is a *rabbi* a leader?

   d What is the difference between a *nation* and an *empire*?

4 Draw a picture or write a short description of a *boxcar*, a *louse* (plural: *lice*), a *swastika*, a *synagogue*.

After you read

5 Find the years for each of these events in Oskar Schindler's life. Explain how his actions or reactions to some of them show hints of a heroic future.

   a He enjoys a summer of professional motorbike racing.

   b He marries Emilie.

   c He agrees to collect information for German military intelligence.

   d He meets Itzhak Stern and Leopold Pfefferberg.

   e He warns Itzhak Stern of the first *Aktion*.

   f DEF begins to get military contracts.

   g Oskar welcomes Edith Liebgold and her friends to DEF.

6 What is Oskar Schindler's relationship to these people, and what influence do thay have on his character and opinions?

Hans Schindler   Rabbi Kantor   Emilie   Eberhard Gebauer
Itzhak Stern   Leopold Pfefferberg   Victoria Klonowska

Chapters 4–6

Before you read

7 Find these words in your dictionary. Explain why each of them was a frightening word to a Jew in Krakow during the Second World War:

barracks   (gas) chamber   commandant   crematorium   disinfect

After you read

8 Who is frightened in these situations? Why?
   a after being arrested and sent to Montelupich prison
   b after being denied a blue stamp
   c sitting on horseback above the ghetto
   d in Belzec death camp
   e in the basement of the old Technical College
   f at Plaszów after Diana Reiter is murdered
   g in Krakow's Jewish ghetto on 13 March 1943

Chapters 7–9

Before you read

9 In Chapter 3, Itzhak Stern says that the ghetto might be the final step the Germans will take against the Jews. Discuss why it is necessary for the Jews to believe this.

10 Find these words in your dictionary:

binoculars   chess   colonel   hinge   liberation   sentence

Which of these is:
   a part of a door?
   b a game?
   c a penalty?
   d used by bird watchers?
   e dreamed of by prisoners?
   f a military position?

11 Why do the prisoners at Plaszów feel afraid when:

    a Commandant Goeth appears on his balcony?

    b Goeth enters one of the camp workshops?

    c the entire population of the camp is required to appear in the main square?

    d a group of prisoners is put into boxcars?

    e there are rumours that DEF will soon be closed?

12 What has Oskar Schindler done to earn 'a hundred bullets for his own head or a trip to Auschwitz' in connection with these people?

    Manasha Levartov   Helen Hirsch   the Danziger brothers

    Adam Garde

Chapters 10–11

Before you read

13 What do you think prisoners will do to get their names on Schindler's list?

14 Look up *tattoo* in your dictionary. What is the word in your language? Where do people in your country usually have tattoos on their bodies? What kind of pictures or words are popular?

After you read

15 Put these four actions of Oskar Schindler in the order in which they happen in the autumn of 1944 and explain the importance of each.

    a He visits the Hoffman Brothers Cloth Factory.

    b He meets Colonel Erich Lange in Berlin.

    c He passes the list to Commandant Büscher at Plaszów.

    d He has his first meeting with engineer Sussmuth.

16 What route do the men and then the women on Schindler's list follow on their journeys from Plaszów to Brinnlitz? Why is it surprising that any of them arrive there alive?

17 Answer these questions about the story.

    a Why is Amon Goeth arrested?

    b Why is Marcel Goldberg called 'Lord of the Lists'?

    c Why does Commandant Hassebroeck enjoy his visits to the DEF sub-camp at Brinnlitz?

    d Why does Emilie move into Oskar's Brinnlitz apartment?

e How does Oskar get out of jail the third time?

f How does one of Oskar's secretaries help get the Schindler women out of Auschwitz-Birkenau?

g How do Manci Rosner and Regina Horowitz make contact with their sons and husbands before leaving Auschwitz?

h Why do the sons and husbands show their tattoos to Manci and Regina?

Chapters 12–14

Before you read

18 The DEF workers are now in Brinnlitz with Herr Schindler. Do you think their troubles have ended? Why (not)?

19 Look up *typhoid* in your dictionary. What are the signs of this fever? How do people get it?

After you read

20 Why are these things expensive for Oskar Schindler?

a the threat of typhoid fever

b factory inspections by Nazi officials

c the first night after the war ends, in a town jail

21 Work with a partner. Discuss the main points of the two speeches Schindler makes on 28 April and 8 May 1945.

22 List the places Oskar Schindler visits or lives in from the time he leaves Brinnlitz on 8 May 1945 until his death on 9 October 1974. What is significant about each place?

Writing

23 Write a conversation between Leopold Pfefferberg and his grandson. Begin the conversation with the grandson asking, 'Grandpa, what did you do in the Second World War?'

24 You are Emilie Schindler, and Oskar has just visited you for Easter week, 1941. Write a letter to your husband explaining what you had hoped for when you married him and what you are unhappy about in your marriage now.

25 You are Itzhak Stern in 1943. Make a list of the things you will include in the report about Plaszów that Oskar has persuaded you to write for Dr Sedlacek.

26 Describe the personality of one of these people:
Hans Schindler, Itzhak Stern, Leopold Pfefferberg,
Victoria Klonowska, Amon Goeth, Mietek Pemper, Helen Hirsch.

27 Make a list of Oskar Schindler's strengths and weaknesses and
then try to explain why our hero, as Emilie says, 'has done nothing
special since the war.'

28 Write a letter to the head teacher of your local secondary school
giving reasons why this book should be read by every student
who is studying twentieth-century history.